Clemus Romanus Gregg, John Allen Fitzgerald

The Epistle of St. Clement

Bishop of Rome

Clemus Romanus Gregg, John Allen Fitzgerald

The Epistle of St. Clement
Bishop of Rome

ISBN/EAN: 9783744665681

Printed in Europe, USA, Canada, Australia, Japan

Cover: Foto ©Lupo / pixelio.de

More available books at **www.hansebooks.com**

PREFACE

It may safely be said that, with the exception of the New Testament, no piece of literature belonging to the early Church stands on so secure a foundation, as regards external attestation and MS. authority, as does the Epistle of Clement. But when we say this, we are saying what could not have been said twenty-five years ago. At that time there was but one MS., which was known to contain this Epistle, and even then, owing to the loss of an entire leaf in the original, scholars were in total ignorance of what we now possess as §§ 58-64. Now we have four MSS. of first-rate authority, standing side by side, and pointing to independent lines of tradition. These correct, supplement, or corroborate one another in such a way that the restored text of this Epistle may be said to represent the original autograph more closely and with more certainty than is possible in the case of any other classical or patristic work.

The question of the authorship of the Epistle is one merely of literary interest, and can be approached only from outside. Whether Clement was the writer or not, it makes no difference; the Epistle was certainly in the hands of Polycarp, who wrote his Epistle early in the second century, and of Hegesippus and Irenæus, who wrote about 180 A.D. The Epistle itself lays no claim to being the work of any individual; it is an exhortation from the Church sojourning at Rome to the Church at Corinth; but in spite of the fact that the name of Clement is not once mentioned, and the office of Bishop of Rome is not even hinted at, the consensus of later testimony points to a widespread tradition assigning its authorship to Clement, Bishop of Rome.

Like the works of the two other Apostolic Fathers, Ignatius and Polycarp, the writing of Clement takes the form of an Epistle.

It is not merely a tract in the form of a letter, like the Epistle of Barnabas, but it was written with a definite purpose, having been called forth by special circumstances. It is one of the few literary remains of the Church of the first century, and considering its antiquity, may chance to be regarded as somewhat disappointing in its contents. But its value is negative rather than positive. If it does not finally dispose of the problems of the early Christian ministry, it refutes as clearly as is possible the Tübingen hypothesis of a rivalry between St. Peter and St. Paul. Not only are the two Apostles held up side by side as examples worthy to be followed, but the letter contains obvious reminiscences of the language of the Epistles of both. Again, although it is plain, from his intimate knowledge of canonical and apocryphal Jewish literature, that the writer has Jewish sympathies, anything like an anti-Pauline tone is entirely absent from his references to St. Paul. "His Judaism is that of the Old Testament, not of the Pharisaic revival. The Jewish Scriptures, not the Jews of the present, are the influence which is at work."

This Epistle presents a striking example of the difference between the canonical and uncanonical books. Though it is one of the two earliest Christian writings which do not claim an Apostle as author, and may be assigned to the same date as the Gospel of St. John, it stands on a lower level of thought, and speaks rather with the appeal of an elder brother than with the authority of a father. The Apostles were originators; Clement did no more than appropriate their teaching: the Apostles laid down the law; Clement expounded it, but added nothing to it.

"His genuine Epistle was never translated into the Latin language; and hence it became a dead letter to the Church over which he presided, when that Church ceased to speak Greek and adopted the vernacular tongue." It is with mingled feelings of pleasure and regret that we can now read these words, which appear in the last edition of Bishop Lightfoot's work, "The Apostolic Fathers" (*Clement of Rome*, vol. i., pp. 98 and 146). The discovery at Namur of an early Latin translation, and its publication in 1894, caused a temporary revival of interest in the Epistle, and it was then seen that, even though the words quoted above would need to be rewritten, some of Bishop Lightfoot's suggestions were fully borne out by this latest accession of evidence. We cannot but regret, however, that the Latin version, which by the discoverer's own admission was known to him even before the publication in 1875 of the Constantinopolitan MS., was kept back from general notice until after the death of one who had made the works of the Apostolic Fathers particularly his own subject.

It would be presumptuous for any editor to attempt to put forward a translation of this Epistle, however simple, without having first studied Bishop Lightfoot's work, *Clement of Rome*, 1890. It is almost true that all that is to be said on the subject has been said by him; and consequently, likenesses to his work, conscious or unconscious, may be continually traced throughout the translation and notes in this book. Where possible, all debts to him or to other writers have been acknowledged. It only remains to be added that the design of this edition is to place in the hands of uncritical readers the Epistle of Clement in the most simple form, and to offer such explanations in the notes as may be required for the sake of either illustrating the text or showing the use that has been made of the Latin Version. This is the first edition, as far as the editor is aware, in which the evidence offered by the recently discovered version has been employed.

An expression of gratitude is due to Canon (late Professor) Armitage Robinson, who generously placed his introductory notes on the Epistle at the editor's disposal; also to Mr. J. Rendel Harris, for assistance kindly rendered by him in connection with the Latin version.

THE
EPISTLE OF ST. CLEMENT

I. Date.

THE evidence points to 96 A.D. as the date of the Epistle. If we may accept Bishop Lightfoot's conclusion that the Epistle of Polycarp was written between 110 A.D. and 120 A.D., we have at once an inferior limit for the date of our own Epistle, inasmuch as the Epistle of Polycarp "is pervaded through and through with indications of a knowledge of Clement's letter." The latest date suggested by critics of the most advanced school was the reign of Hadrian, and this is put out of court by the argument from the Epistle of Polycarp. It remains for us to decide between the earliest suggested date, about 67 A.D., and that which is by far the most widely supported, 95 or 96 A.D.

If external evidence is to be trusted, and we are to be guided by the tradition (dating from as early as Hegesippus and Dionysius of Corinth, 170 A.D.) that Clement was the writer of the Epistle, then we must accept the later of the two dates. Eusebius (*Hist. Eccl.* iii. 34) tells us that Clement died in the third year of Trajan (101 A.D.), after having held office for nine years. External evidence has thus given us 92 A.D. as the earliest, and 101 A.D. as the latest limit; how is this borne out by internal evidence?

The Epistle refers to two periods of persecution, one belonging to the past, in which the Apostles St. Peter and St. Paul suffered, together with many other examples of Christian fortitude (cpp. 5, 6), the other but recently ended.

The first period was not so far removed from the second as to prevent those who suffered in it from being reckoned as "of the same generation" with those who suffered in the preceding one, when set in comparison with Jacob, Joseph, Moses, and David. Now early writers know of two persecutions only in the first century, viz. that of Nero, followed, after an interval of about twenty-five or thirty years, by that of Domitian. When, in addition to this, we remember the almost unquestioned tradition that the two Apostles suffered under Nero, we can hardly hesitate to infer that this Epistle was written immediately after the persecution of Domitian. This persecution is still sufficiently near at hand for the writers to say of themselves that they are "in the same lists with" those earlier sufferers (cp. 7), but nevertheless it is spoken of in the past tense, "the sudden and oft-repeated calamities which *befel* us" (cp. 1). This is made clear by the Latin version, which justifies Lightfoot's retention of γενομένας by translating it "quæ contigerunt." It should be remembered that the latter persecution is characterized by the words "sudden" and "oft-repeated" (cp. 1), words which are quite true when used of a series of capricious attacks, but which would not fairly represent the "war of extermination" set on foot by Nero.

Internal evidence presents another insuperable difficulty in the way of the earlier date. In chapter 44 we read that the Corinthians have deposed from their office certain presbyters, who have been well reported of "for a long time" (πολλοῖς χρόνοις). Fifty-two A.D. is the earliest date at which a local college of presbyters could have been appointed at Corinth, and this expression (πολλοὶ χρόνοι) would be very much exaggerated, if it pointed back to a space of no more than sixteen years. A similar inference may be drawn from chapter 63. The Roman messengers are spoken of as having lived unblamably "from young to old age." If this Epistle were written in 68 A.D., it would be a stretch of imagination to use these words of them, seeing that only ten years previously, the Church in Rome was practically non-existent. The words would have full meaning, if we allow the Epistle to have been written in 96 A.D.

II. The Author.

THERE is nothing whatever in the Epistle itself to indicate Clement as its author; the salutation is addressed to the Church sojourning in Corinth from the Church sojourning in Rome; and the first person plural is employed throughout. The most reasonable supposition is that Clement drafted the letter, and that the Church, although in no way attempting to disguise its authorship, dispatched it in the name and with the authority of the entire Church. It is probable that the literary attainments of the Roman presbyters were not of a very high order, and it would be the most convenient plan, when they desired to join in a letter of protest or counsel, to entrust its preparation to the Bishop, or, if the see was vacant, to the most respected and most talented of their number. This supposition is borne out by the words of Dionysius of Corinth, who wrote about 170 A.D., quoted by Eusebius (*Hist. Eccl.* iv. 23)—"The Epistle written to us through Clement," while Irenæus, who wrote about 180 A.D., is no more explicit, saying merely— "In the time of this Clement, the Church at Rome dispatched a letter" (*Adv. Hær.* iii. 23). That a letter drafted by the Bishop, or one of the presbyters, might be regarded as the letter of the whole Church is plain from various references. In the passage from Eusebius quoted above, Dionysius of Corinth, writing to Soter, Bishop of Rome, refers to a letter written by him as "*your* (plural) letter." Eusebius (v. 24) quotes a letter from Polycrates, a bishop in Asia, who, in answer to a communication from Victor, Bishop of Rome, forwarded in the name of the Roman Church, says, "you (plural) desired." Lastly, among the letters of Cyprian we find one (Ep. xxx.) bearing the heading, "Cypriano papæ presbyteri et diaconi Romæ consistentes," and written throughout in the first person plural. This Epistle, however, was the work of a single individual, Novatian, one of the leading presbyters in the Church at Rome, as is shown by the words of Cyprian in Ep. lv. 5.

Thus, there is nothing to hinder us from accepting the statement of Clement of Alexandria that the Epistle of the Romans to the Corinthians was the work of Clement, Bishop of Rome.

With regard to Clement himself very little is known. Origen identified him with the Clement mentioned in Phil. iv. 3, but the Clement there referred to belongs to Philippi and not to Rome, while (as Lightfoot shows) the name of Clement was very common during the age of the Flavian dynasty. It is possible that reference is made to Clement, Bishop of Rome, in the "Shepherd of Hermas" (*Vis.* ii. 4), where Hermas is instructed to write two books, one of which he is to give to Clement, whose duty it will be to send it to the cities abroad. But various doubtful considerations are involved here, which make the evidence deducible from this passage of very slender value.

We have it on the authority of Irenæus (*Adv. Hær.* iii. 3. 3) that the third Bishop of Rome, after the Apostles St. Peter and St. Paul, was Clement, a man who had seen the Apostles and conversed with them, and who had their preaching in his ears, and their tradition before his eyes. Eusebius (iii. 34) enables us to date his tenure of the see of Rome from 92 A.D. to 101 A.D.

Clement must have been a man of some note, seeing that he became the subject of an early romance, on which were based both the Clementine Homilies and Recognitions; the romance, however, may be dismissed as being valueless for the purpose of evidence. It will suffice to give, in Bishop Lightfoot's own words, the result at which he arrived after a laborious examination of the evidence both of written documents and of the inscriptions in the Catacombs. "I venture to conjecture that Clement the bishop was a man of Jewish descent, a freedman or the son of a freedman belonging to the house of Flavius Clemens, the cousin of Domitian (*Clement of Rome*, vol. i. p. 61), whom the Emperor put to death for his profession of Christianity."

If we accept Clement as author of the Epistle, we can have little hesitation in asserting that he was brought up among Jewish surroundings. The Old Testament is his Bible, while the New Testament, although he shows acquaintance with its language and spirit, occupies quite a subordinate position in his mind. The Old Testament supplies him with numerous lengthy quotations, on which he bases much of his argument.

III. The Epistle.

(*a*) *Its purpose.* Corinth stood midway between east and west. It was a halting-place for travellers on their way from Asia Minor or Syria to Rome. As there was a close connection between the Roman residents there and the mother city, so there is no doubt that the Churches at Corinth and Rome were linked together by ties equally strong. It would thus cause no small anxiety to the Roman Church, when news was brought that there was a serious division in the Church of Corinth.

Certain ringleaders of sedition, having secured a considerable following, had contrived the deposition of some of the presbyters who held their office by direct transmission from the Apostles, and whose life was free from the slightest taint of suspicion. This internal discord had doubtless caused the Church to be forgetful of its duties towards travelling members of other Churches, and the magnitude of the evil would not be underrated on the arrival at Rome of those who had landed at Corinth with the hope of enjoying the well-known hospitality of its Church, and had gone on their way aggrieved at the neglectful treatment they had received.

The tone of chapter 1 leads us to conclude that news of the faction reached Rome through private channels, and was not communicated officially. While exaggeration on the part of the informers was not wanting, as the words "that unholy and impious sedition" show, there is no hint in the Greek that any letter applying for advice or arbitration had been addressed to the Church at Rome. The Roman letter was dictated by feelings of affection towards a sister Church; it was an act of interference which the Roman presbyters did not attempt to justify by an appeal to any supposed superior authority, being nothing more than the plain duty of one member of the Body of Christ towards another who is palpably in the wrong. It appealed for a speedy settlement of the dispute; it did not attempt to command. It may be that the Roman presbyters wrote because they were conscious that their Church held a position of supreme responsibility owing both to its situation in the Imperial city, and to its twofold Apostolic foundation; but, however that may be, their words did not claim to derive their weight from any authority residing in the person of the successor of St. Peter.

It is noteworthy that the two main points in this Epistle are the same as those which occupied St. Paul's attention in his first Epistle to the same Church, viz. the Resurrection and the evils of division. Whether the doctrine of the Resurrection had been perverted by heretical teachers, or whether the general attitude of the Corinthian Church towards it had been one of sceptical indifference, we have no means of judging; it must have been some urgent cause that called forth the apologetic statement which we find here.

The dangers of division may, roughly speaking, be said to be treated under three heads. (1) The evil results of jealousy, as proved by examples from the Old Testament and elsewhere; (2) the value of order, to which Nature bears striking witness; (3) the blessings of concord, and the Christian duty of submissiveness and meekness.

(*b*) *Its result.* We are not informed as to the result of the Roman appeal. The first account that we possess of the state of the Church at Corinth in later times comes from Hegesippus, who, writing about A.D. 170, tells how the Corinthian Church continued in the right doctrine until the time of Primus, Bishop of Corinth. Half a century at least must have elapsed between the time of the writing of the Roman Epistle and the visit of Hegesippus.

(*c*) *Analysis of its contents.*

§§ 1, 2. The Corinthian Church has belied its reputation for hospitality and submissiveness of disposition.

§§ 3–6. The dangers of jealousy, and its consequences for Abel, Jacob, Joseph, Moses, Aaron, David, St. Peter, and St. Paul, and the sufferers in the persecution of Nero.

§§ 7, 8. The need of repentance.

§§ 9–12. Examples to be followed. — Enoch the obedient, Noah the preacher of righteousness, Abraham the faithful, Lot rewarded for his piety and hospitality, Rahab rewarded for her faith and hospitality.

§§ 13–18. The need of humility and peaceableness. § 16. Christ is an example; so (§ 17) are the prophets Elijah, Elisha, and Ezekiel; so are Abraham, Job, Moses, (§ 18) David.

§§ 19–23. The peace and long-suffering of God crowns the humility of men. § 20. Heaven, earth, ocean, seasons, winds, springs, and animals, submit to law and observe due order. § 21. Surely, then, men should live in concord and humility, as (§ 22) our Christian faith testifies. § 23. God is merciful and gracious; let us not waver or doubt the sincerity of His purposes. One day He will come suddenly.

§§ 24–27. The Resurrection. Nature bears witness to it. §§ 25, 26. Analogy from the phœnix. § 27. We should fix our hopes on the Resurrection.

§§ 28–36. God's eye is everywhere; let us, therefore, put away evil desires. § 29. Let us lift up holy hands to Him. § 30. We are members of a holy fellowship, therefore let us be holy. We need concord, humility, self-control, both in body and tongue, and reasonableness (ἐπιείκεια is one of the key-words of the Epistle). § 31. The way to win the blessing of God, as shown by Abraham, Isaac, and Jacob. § 32. God's will is the source of blessing, not the works of man's righteousness; faith alone brings a man into touch with the Divine will. § 33. But faith does not involve idleness: God rejoices in His works, and therein we have an example for ourselves. § 34. We must not be weary in well-doing, but we must aim at unity and concord, if we are to partake of God's promises in their fullest measure. § 35. They are worth winning, therefore let us forego all wranglings and selfish pride. § 36. Christ will be on our side, and will open our eyes, and reveal to us heavenly secrets.

§§ 37-48. We are like an army, there must be subordination of rank; we are like the human body, there must be co-operation. § 38. The need of helpfulness and submissiveness in all. § 39. Self-exaltation is folly, and is condemned by the Word of God. §§ 40, 41. God demands order in everything; He has shown His will by the institution of special times of sacrifice, and special ministers to attend at the altar. § 42. The apostles were commissioned in due order by Christ; Christ was duly sent forth from God. The apostles, having regard to order, instituted the offices of bishop (*i.e.* presbyter) and deacon. § 43. They followed the example set by Moses; the settlement of the dispute concerning the priesthood by the laying up of the rods in the tabernacle. § 44. The apostles endeavoured to guard against such disputes, and provided for a due succession of ministers in the Church. It is a grievous sin to depose blameless men who hold the Apostolic commission. § 45. When the saints were persecuted, *e.g.* Daniel or the Three Children, it was not at the hands of the people of God that they suffered. § 46. Let us remember these examples, and be warned. The deadly nature of schism. § 47. St. Paul reproved the same failing, and perhaps there was then a slight excuse, but none now. § 48. Let us ask for pardon; the indispensableness of humility.

§§ 49–59. The love of God, and the need and blessings of love in man, to which the Word of God bears witness. § 51. Hardness of heart will bring ruin to us as it did to Pharaoh. § 52. God can be enriched by man with nothing but the sacrifice of praise and confession. §§ 53, 54. The self-forgetfulness of Moses should be an example to the ringleaders, encouraging them to give way. § 55. Heathen kings have given proof of their devotion; look also at Esther and Judith, besides other noble women. § 56. We must pray that a spirit of reasonableness may be given to the Church. §§ 57–59. A final appeal to the ringleaders, followed by the warnings of the first chapter of the Book of Proverbs. An exhortation to the Church at large to be reasonable: the writers have done their best.

§§ 59–61. An early prayer for the Church militant.

§§ 62–64. The teaching of the Epistle is summed up. In a godly life there must be faith, repentance, love, temperateness, patience, but together with these there must be concord, peace, and "determined reasonableness." § 63. The past is our lesson-book. You will give us joy if you will listen to our entreaties. § 64. May God grant us all that our souls need.

§ 65. Commendation of the messengers who carry the Epistle.

IV. External Testimony.

POLYCARP OF SMYRNA does not mention the Epistle, but he does what is better for our purpose. He shows an unmistakable acquaintance with the phraseology of the Epistle, echoes of which appear everywhere in his Epistle to the Philippians.

HEGESIPPUS, writing about 170 A.D., mentions the Epistle of Clement to the Corinthians (Eus. *H. E.* iv. 22).

DIONYSIUS OF CORINTH, writing about the same time, mentions that it was an established custom of many years' standing to read the Epistle of Clement in the Church on the Lord's Day (Eus. *H. E.* iv. 23).

IRENÆUS, writing about ten years later, mentions the ἱκανωτάτη γραφή—the weighty letter, which was dispatched by the Roman to the Corinthian Church in the days of Clement (*Adv. Hær.* iii. 3. 3).

EUSEBIUS, the Historian, writes (*H. E.* iii. 16) that it was becoming very common for the Epistle of Clement to be read in the Churches.

V. Manuscripts, etc.

UNTIL the year 1875 the Alexandrian MS. (usually known as A), in the British Museum, was the solitary witness to the text of the Epistle; it is by far the oldest, and (although not quite complete) the most authoritative of all our extant *codices* of the Epistle. But in that year Philotheus Bryennius, then Metropolitan of Serræ, published in a volume of quite sensational interest for scholars, the transcription of a MS. which he had discovered at Constantinople, containing amongst other things the hitherto unknown text of the "TEACHING OF THE APOSTLES," and a new and independent text of the Epistle of Clement. The Alexandrian MS., which is written in uncial characters, may be roughly assigned to the year 400 A.D., while that from Constantinople (better known as C) bears its own date, 1056 A.D. These two MSS. are independent, and therefore must be traced back to an archetype earlier (and probably considerably earlier) than 400 A.D.

In the same year the Cambridge University Library secured a MS., containing Syriac versions of the greater portion of the New Testament, and of the Epistle of St. Clement. This new authority (known as S) is very useful for throwing light on places where C differs from A, but it suffers from all the disadvantages of such a translation. There are, however, some passages where it preserves the true reading, which has been lost in both the Greek MSS. This MS., in its turn, exhibits a text entirely independent of A and C, and would probably compel us to go back as far as the beginning of the third, or even the end of the second century, if we sought for the date of the archetype from which all three might trace their descent.

These three MSS., supplemented by occasional quotations in Clement of Alexandria, constituted the entire *apparatus criticus* available until the year 1894, when the Latin version (known as L) was published by D. G. Morin, O.S.B., of the monastery of Maredsous in Belgium. This version was contained in a well-written MS. of the tenth or eleventh century, and had belonged originally to the monastery of Florennes, whence it was transferred to the library of the Great Seminary at Namur. It is published in what promises to be a very valuable series of texts, *Anecdota Maredsolana*. This text presents variations of so important a character, that we can only conclude that we possess in it a fourth independent witness to an archetype of the second or third century.

The question naturally arises, "What was the origin and date of this version?" It was not the work of Jerome, for a comparison between the few fragments of a translation by him and the corresponding portions of the version shows that there is no connection between the work of the two translators. Moreover, the quotations are rendered into Latin of a pre-Hieronymian type.

If we may accept Professor Sanday's inference (*Guardian*, March 28, 1894) that this version was known to St. Ambrose, we are carried back within the limits of the fourth century at latest. Dr. Harnack (*Theolog. Literatur.*, March 17, 1894) would assign a very early date to the version : he argues that there were two great periods of translation in the history of the early Church, the first between 150 and 250, and the second from the end of the fourth to shortly after the beginning of the fifth century, and, guided by the linguistic evidence, he unhesitatingly dates it about 200 A.D. Professor Sanday, who differs from Dr. Harnack in thinking better of the Latinity and worse of the text, pronounces in favour of 200—350 A.D. as the period during which the translation was made. It is quite plain from obvious corruptions belonging to the Latin text itself that the translation is a great deal older than the text found at Namur; while a proof of the value of its testimony may be found in the fact that, in the case of various quotations occurring in Clement of Alexandria, while A and C have since become corrupted, the Latin text agrees with the reading of Clement, thus preserving the original reading of the archetype from which the quotation was made. There is no need to give here any examples of the variations or corrections supplied by L: the attention of the reader has been directed in the notes to the most important, as they occur in the order of the text.

VI. Canonicity.

THE question of the Canonicity of the Epistle may be said to be beyond the range of dispute. The fact that it was read in the Church, both at Corinth and in many other places, proves nothing; the same honour was promised to the Epistle of Soter, more than half a century later. The language of the Fathers of the second and third centuries, and their attitude towards the Epistle of Clement, are plain proof that they regarded it as standing on an entirely different level to the books of apostolic authorship. The historian, Eusebius, writing at the beginning of the fourth century, does not even rank it (*H. E.* vi. 14) with the "disputed" books which include the Epistle of Jude, the remaining Catholic Epistles, the Epistle of Barnabas, and the so-called Revelation of Peter. In the Alexandrian MS. of the New Testament (A), it comes after the Revelation of St. John, thus as late as the fifth century ranking among apocryphal books.

TO THE CORINTHIANS.

THE Church of God[1] sojourning[2] in Rome to the Church of God sojourning in Corinth, to them that are called[3] and sanctified by the will of God through our Lord Jesus Christ. Grace to you and peace from Almighty God through Jesus Christ be multiplied.

I. By reason of the sudden and oft-repeated calamities and troubles which have befallen us,[4] brethren, we con-

---

[1] This anonymous salutation is copied by the elders of Smyrna, in their letter to the Church at Philomelium, describing the Passion of Polycarp; it should be contrasted with the salutation of Polycarp's own letter to the Philippians, which begins, "Polycarp and the presbyters that are with him."

[2] Sojourning ($\pi\alpha\rho o\iota\kappa o\hat{\upsilon}\sigma\alpha$). This word recalls 1 Pet. i. 17, "Pass the time of your sojourning here in fear" ($\pi\alpha\rho o\iota\kappa\iota\alpha$); also 1 Pet. ii. 11, "I beseech you as strangers" ($\pi\alpha\rho o\iota\kappa o\upsilon\varsigma$). The Church was contemplated as "sojourning" in the heathen world from two points of view; first, because its religious beliefs and moral standards differed entirely from all those in the midst of which Christians had to live; and secondly, because the life on earth is regarded merely as one stage in the journey to a heavenly country.

[3] Cf. 1 Cor. i. 2, "To them that are sanctified in Christ Jesus, called to be saints."

[4] Sudden, because the attacks made by Domitian were intermittent: the minds of the Roman presbyters had been distracted by their uncertainty as to when and where the next blow would fall. This word characterizes well the persecution under Domitian, which was quite different from the general attack made by Nero. Eusebius (*H. E.* iii. 17) tells us that Domitian, often quite apart from religious reasons, banished many Roman nobles and confiscated their property. Among these was Domitian's first cousin, Flavius Clemens, the consul in A.D. 95, who was executed. This Clemens married Flavia Domitilla, niece of the Emperor. Eusebius (*H. E.* iii. 18) writes that she

sider [1] that we have been slow in turning our attention to the questions in dispute among you,[2] beloved, and to that disgraceful and unholy division, which is so alien to the spirit of the elect of God, and yet has been kindled by a few headstrong and reckless persons to such a pitch of folly, that it has caused very evil things to be spoken of your name, once so widely honoured and so rightly beloved of all men.

For who ever sojourned among you and did not prove the virtuousness and firmness of your faith? or marvelled not at the sobriety and respectfulness of your Christian piety? or did not tell of your noble disposition of hospitality? or failed to congratulate you on your perfect and unshaken knowledge?[3]

All that ye did was without respect of persons; ye walked after the ordinances of God; ye submitted yourselves to your rulers,[4] and ye paid the honour that was due to the older men among you. Upon the young men ye enjoined sober and seemly thoughts; the women ye exhorted to fulfil all their duties with a blameless and seemly and pure conscience, rendering to their own husbands the

---

was exiled on account of her profession of Christianity. As she would probably be a leading figure in the Church at Rome, this may be one of the sudden calamities referred to.

[1] The Latin version reads "uidemur," which indicates in the original, νομιζόμεθα, "we seem to have been slow."

[2] This expression is generally interpreted to mean that no official request for mediation had been conveyed from the Corinthian to the Roman Church, but that the Roman letter was based upon casual reports, brought perhaps by travellers. The Latin version, however, which gives "de quibus desideratis," implies clearly that the Roman Church had been consulted.

[3] Knowledge (γνῶσις) is one of the central words of the two Epistles of St. Paul to the Corinthians, cf. 1 Cor. i. 5, "In everything ye are enriched by Him, in all utterance, and in all knowledge."

[4] *i.e.* to your rulers in the Church: the word is the same as in Heb. xiii. 7, "Remember them which have the rule over you."

love that was due to them; and ye taught them that they should observe the rule of obedience, and perform their household tasks with seemliness and wise discretion.

II. And ye were all humble-minded and unassuming, willing to submit rather than claiming submission, finding it greater joy *to give than to receive* (cf. Acts xx. 35), satisfied with the sustenance[1] that Christ can give. Moreover, ye gave heed to His words and laid them diligently to heart, while His sufferings were ever before your eyes.

Thus was there granted to all a deep and rich peace, and a fervent desire to do good; and the Holy Spirit was shed forth upon you all in abundant measure. So, being full of holy counsel, with a noble zeal and pious confidence ye stretched forth your hands unto Almighty God, intreating Him to be propitious, if ye had unwittingly fallen into sin.

Ye had conflict day and night for all the brotherhood,[2] that the number of His elect might be saved by their

---

[1] Lightfoot urges in a long note that ἐφόδια means provisions *bodily*, not spiritual, and cites Eusebius (*H. E.* iv. 23) who quotes part of a letter from Dionysius, bishop of Corinth, to Soter, bishop of Rome (c. 160 A.D.), in which this word occurs twice, with reference to supplies sent from the Roman to the Corinthian Church at a time of great need. This view was taken by Lightfoot, who accepted the reading of A (ἐφοδίοις Θεοῦ) against C and S (ἐφ. Χριστοῦ). The Latin version however gives its testimony against A, and therefore we must accept the reading rejected by Lightfoot, "alimentis Christi." He admits that ἐφόδια bears not unfrequently the sense of spiritual sustenance; and further, the idea of spiritual support afforded by Christ supplies a pointed antithesis to the preceding words, "finding it greater joy to give than to receive." Again, it cannot be denied that it is more natural to speak of the sufferings of *Christ*, in the following clause (where the text gives "His sufferings"), than of the "sufferings of *God*," although, as Lightfoot says, the Catholic doctrine of the Person of Christ admits both ways of speaking.

[2] Here, as in 1 Pet. ii. 17, ἀδελφότης has the concrete sense of a band of brothers.

compassion[1] and intentness. Ye were sincere and upright and forgiving towards one another. Ye detested any division or schism.[2] Ye were as vexed at the transgressions of your neighbours, as if ye judged their failures to be your own. Any good deed of yours was without repentance, ye were *ready to every good work* (Titus iii. 1). Ye were adorned with a virtuous and excellent manner of life, and the fear of God governed all your actions: the commandments and ordinances of the Lord *were written on the tables of your hearts* (cf. Prov. vii. 3).

III. All glory and increase[3] were given unto you, and that which was written was brought to pass. *My beloved ate and drank and was increased and grew thick and kicked.*[4] This is the source of jealousy and envy, wrath and division, persecution and disorder, war and captivity. This is how *the base* rise up *against the honourable*, the men of no repute against them that are well reputed, the fools against the wise, *the young men against their elders* (Is. iii. 5). For this cause *righteousness standeth aloof* (Is. lix. 14) and peace, while every man leaves the fear of God because his faith in Him has become dim: he walks

---

[1] Lightfoot, on the inferior authority of C (which reads μετὰ δέους, for μετ' ἐλέους found in A and S), translated "that they might be saved with fearfulness," and found here a close parallel to Heb. xii. 28, "Serve God with reverence and awe" (R.V.). But the Latin version gives "cum misericordia," and thus supports directly A and S. The words, "compassion and intentness," will now refer to those Corinthians who interceded for the brotherhood, their compassion being shown by their brotherly kindness towards offenders (Zahn), and their intentness by their prayers day and night. "Intentness" is Lightfoot's translation of συνείδησις, which, he says, "denotes inward concentration and assent."

[2] Cf. 1 Cor. xi. 18. St. Paul's reproofs had evidently borne lasting fruit.

[3] Increase, lit. "broadening of circumstances." The Greek word conveys exactly the opposite sense to that of the word which in 2 Cor. iv. 8, is translated "distressed," which is literally "narrowed."

[4] A very free quotation from the Septuagint of Deut. xxxii. 14.

not in the ordinances of His commandments and lives not in the way that is meet for a Christian. Not one but follows the lusts of his evil heart, and has conceived a godless and wicked jealousy, through which it was that *death entered into the world* (Wisdom ii. 24).

IV. For thus it is written,[1] *And in process of time it came to pass that Cain brought of the fruits of the earth a sacrifice to God. And Abel, he also brought of the firstlings of the sheep and of their fatness. And God looked upon Abel and his gifts, but Cain and his sacrifices He heeded not. And Cain was troubled exceedingly, and his countenance fell. And God said unto Cain, " Why art thou sore troubled, and why did thy countenance fall? If thou didst offer aright*[2] *but didst not divide aright, didst thou not sin? Be silent: unto thee shall he turn, and thou shalt rule over him." And Cain said unto Abel his brother, " Let us pass over unto the plain."*[3] *And it came to pass that while they were in the plain Cain rose up against Abel his brother and slew him.*

Ye see, brethren, how jealousy and envy made Cain kill his brother. It was by reason of jealousy that Jacob our father fled from the face of Esau his brother. Jealousy it was that caused Joseph to be persecuted to the death, and to enter even into bondage. Jealousy it was that obliged Moses to escape from the face of Pharaoh, king of Egypt, when he heard his fellow-countryman say,

---

[1] This passage is a very close reproduction of the Septuagint of Gen. iv. 3—8.

[2] "The meaning of the original is obscure, but the LXX. translation which Clement here follows must be wrong" (Lightfoot). The translators probably intended the word "divide" to refer to the offence of Cain in keeping the best for himself and devoting the worst to God.

[3] These words are wanting in the Hebrew text. There is good evidence to indicate that these or like words belong to the earliest form of the original.

"*Who made thee a ruler and a judge over us? Wilt thou kill me, as thou diddest the Egyptian yesterday?*" (Ex. ii. 14). It was by reason of jealousy that Aaron and Miriam were made to dwell outside the camp. Jealousy it was that brought down Dathan and Abiram *quick into the pit* (Ps. lv. 16), because they divided themselves against Moses the servant of God. Jealousy it was that caused David to be envied by the aliens,[1] and also to be persecuted by Saul the king of Israel.

V. But enough of examples from the days of old. Let us come to those great ones who are nearest to our time—let us take the grand examples which our own generation supplies.

It was for jealousy and envy that the greatest and most righteous pillars[2] (of the Church) were persecuted and fought even to the death. Let us set before our eyes the good Apostles; Peter,[3] who for unrighteous jealousy submitted to not one, nor two, but many labours, and who having thus borne witness,[4] passed to the appointed

---

[1] The aliens, *i.e.* the Philistines. The Latin version reads, "by his brothers."

[2] Cf. Gal. ii. 9, "James, Cephas, and John, who seemed to be pillars." The Latin version reads, "the most able pillars of the Church."

[3] St. Peter and St. Paul are perhaps selected, owing to the tradition common to the Churches of Rome and Corinth, which told how they first visited Corinth, and then passed into Italy. Eusebius (*H. E.* ii. 25) gives an extract from a letter of Dionysius of Corinth, which, prefaced by his own comment, runs as follows: "That they both suffered martyrdom at the same time, is set forth plainly by Dionysius, bishop of Corinth, in his letter to the Romans—'Herein by your admonition ye have joined together the trees of the Romans and Corinthians, first planted by Peter and Paul. For both of them came alike to our Corinth and planted our Church and taught us; and together they both alike went to Italy, where they first taught and then suffered martyrdom at the same time.'"

[4] Borne witness (μαρτυρήσας): although the sense of μαρτυρεῖν was not confined to *dying* for the faith until many years later, yet the use of the same word by Dionysius in the extract quoted in the preceding

place of glory: Paul, who by reason of jealousy and envy was able to point by his example to the prize of patience.[1] Seven times was he thrown into prison; he was driven into exile,[2] he was stoned; then when he had preached in the East and the West,[3] he attained the noble renown which his faith won for him, teaching righteousness to the whole world, and coming to the furthest limits of the West.[4] Lastly, he bore witness before rulers, and thus passed from the world, and went to the holy place, after proving himself a marvellous pattern of patience.

VI. To these men of holy conversation we must add a goodly company of elect souls who gathered round them, and who, when by reason of jealousy they were subjected to countless indignities and tortures, stood forth as a noble example among us.[5] It was by reason of jealousy that women were persecuted, and were subjected, under the guise of Danaids and Dirces,[6] to

---

note, shows clearly what was the prevailing view as to St. Peter's death. Eusebius in the same chapter quotes Tertullian as his authority for the actual manner of his death, viz. empalement.

[1] Prize. St. Paul uses the same word ($\beta\rho\alpha\beta\epsilon\hat{\iota}o\nu$), Phil. iii. 14, "I press toward the mark for the prize of the high calling of God."

[2] Exile. Under this heading might come his escape from Damascus (2 Cor. xi. 33), and from Jerusalem to Tarsus (Acts ix. 30).

[3] i.e. in Asia and in Europe.

[4] Probably Spain. Great controversy has arisen over these words, but it is hard to see how, in view of the limited knowledge of geography in A.D. 100, the natural sense of the words could be otherwise explained; cf. Romans xv. 24.

[5] Among us, i.e. at Rome. These, as being contemporaries of the Apostles, would be some of Nero's victims.

[6] If we accept the testimony of the MSS., we must imagine that, according to Nero's plan of causing his victims to impersonate the famous sufferers of legend, women were tied by the hair and dragged along by bulls, after the manner of Dirce; but it is in connection with "Danaids" that the difficulty of the passage arises. For although the Danaids were condemned to pass eternity in the fruitless labour of pouring water into a sieve, yet that could hardly

dreadful and unholy violence, until they won the goal for which their faith had struggled, and they received, despite their feebleness, a noble prize. Jealousy it is that alienates wives from their husbands, and reverses the words of our father Adam, *This is now bone of my bones and flesh of my flesh* (Gen. ii. 23). Jealousy and strife have caused the destruction of great cities and the utter overthrow of great nations.

VII. We write thus, beloved, thinking not merely to admonish you but to quicken our own memory. For we are all in the same lists, and the same conflict is before us all. Therefore, let us cease from vain and useless thoughts, and let us approach the glorious and exalted rule that has come down to us, and let us see what is comely and pleasant and acceptable in the sight of our Maker. Let us fix our gaze on the blood of Christ, and let us learn how precious it is unto His Father, because it was shed for our salvation, and won for all the world the grace of repentance. Let us pass on to consider all the generations of men, and observe how in each successive generation the Master[1] has given a place for repentance to those who seek to turn to Him. Noah preached repentance, and all who heeded him were saved. Jonah preached destruction to the men of Nineveh, and they repented of their sins, and propitiated

---

be a form of torture likely to gratify the taste of Nero. And so Wordsworth's emendation, which is one of the most felicitous in the history of textual emendation, has found many supporters; it would read thus when translated—"It was by reason of jealousy that women, girls, and handmaids were persecuted and were subjected, etc." The original reading, however, is supported by the new Latin version, which reads, " Danaides et Dircæ" plainly.

[1] The idea of the Father as " Master " is not frequent in New Testament writers. "Friends, not servants" tells of a higher truth. But here the duty of "subjection" is being impressed upon the Corinthians.

God with their supplications and were saved, aliens[1] though they were from God.

VIII. The ministers of the grace of God[2] spoke through the Holy Spirit concerning repentance, yes, and the Master of all things Himself spoke concerning repentance with an oath: *As I live, saith the Lord, I desire not the death of the sinner, but rather his repentance* (Ezek. xxxiii. 11), adding thereto a goodly counsel, *Repent ye, O house of Israel, of your wickedness. Say unto the sons of my people, " Though your sins reach from earth to heaven,*[3] *and though they be redder than scarlet and blacker than sackcloth, if ye turn unto Me with a whole heart and say 'Father,' I will hearken unto you as unto a holy people."*

And in another place He saith, *Wash you and make you clean. Put away your iniquities from your souls before My eyes. Cease from your iniquities; learn to do well; seek out judgment; deliver the oppressed; give judgment for the orphan and uphold the cause of the widow. And come, saith He, and let us reason together. Though your sins be as crimson, I will make them white as snow, and though they be as scarlet, I will make them white as wool. And if ye be willing and give ear unto Me, ye shall eat the good things of the earth; but if ye be not willing and give not ear unto Me, a sword shall eat you up; for the mouth of the Lord hath spoken it.* We see then how He seeks that all His beloved should have part in

---

[1] Like all Gentiles, they were aliens from the commonwealth of Israel. Eph. ii. 12.

[2] Perhaps a reminiscence of 2 Peter i. 21, where, in connection with prophecy, we are told that men spake from God through the Holy Spirit.

[3] Lightfoot suggests that Clement is quoting throughout this passage from an apocryphal writing ascribed to Ezekiel, rather than that he is fusing different passages from the Psalms, Jeremiah, and Isaiah.

repentance, and how He established it by His omnipotent will.

IX. And so let us give heed to His great and glorious will, and let us fall like suppliants before His mercy and kindness; let us cease from futile toil and strife and the jealousy that leads to death, and throw ourselves upon His mercies. Let us fix our gaze on those who ministered perfectly unto His excellent glory.[1] Enoch, for example, who was found righteous in his obedience and was translated, so that his death was not found. Noah, being found faithful, by his ministration preached a regeneration for the world,[2] and the Master employed him in saving the creatures that entered without confusion[3] into the ark.

X. Abraham, who was called "the friend,"[4] was found faithful, in that he obeyed the words of God. In obedience, he went out from his country and his kindred and his father's house, in order that by leaving a narrow country and a weakly kindred and a meagre house he might inherit the promises of God. For He saith unto him: *Get thee out from thy country and thy kindred and thy father's house unto the land that I show thee, and I will make thee into a great nation, and I will bless thee and will magnify thy name, and thou shalt be blessed. And I will bless them that bless thee, and I will curse them that curse thee, and in thee shall all the kindreds of the earth be blessed* (Gen. xii. 1—3). And again, when he had severed himself from Lot, God said unto him, *Lift up thine eyes and look from the place where now thou art, to the north and the south and the sunrising and the*

---
[1] This expression occurs in 2 Pet. i. 17.
[2] *i.e.* after the Flood.
[3] This is a subtle allusion to the confusion existing at Corinth, which is reproved even by the dumb animals.
[4] Is. xli. 8, "Abraham my friend."

sea : for all the land which thou seest, to thee will I give it and to thy seed for ever. And I will make thy seed as the dust of the earth : if a man can number the dust of the earth, then shall thy seed be numbered (Gen. xiii. 14—16). And again he saith, *God brought Abraham forth and spake unto him: lift up thine eyes to heaven and tell the stars, if thou shalt be able to number them. So shall thy seed be. And Abraham believed God, and it was reckoned unto him for righteousness* (Gen. xv. 5, 6). His faith and his hospitality[1] won for him a son in his old age, and in obedience he offered that son as a sacrifice to God on one of the mountains which He had shown him.

XI. For his hospitality and his piety Lot was allowed to escape from Sodom, when the whole country round about was judged with fire and brimstone. Thus did the Master show forth that, while He forsakes not them that hope in Him, He visits with punishment and pain such as turn aside. For Lot's wife, who went forth with him, but wavered in her heart and consented not with him,[2] was made a pillar of salt unto this day, that she might be a sign, to the effect that all might know that the double-minded and they that doubt concerning the power of God are appointed for a judgment and a warning to all generations.

XII. For her faith and her hospitality, Rahab the harlot found safety. For when the spies were sent forth into Jericho by Joshua the son of Nun, the king of the

---

[1] Hospitality had been one of the virtues of the Corinthian Church, cf. § 2. Perhaps complaints of inhospitable treatment had been made by travellers reaching Rome from the East against the Corinthian Church, which had been too much occupied with its own dissensions to attend to the needs of strangers. In this way the Roman letter may have been drawn forth as much for the sake of the Church generally, as of the Church in Corinth.

[2] Again, an allusion to Corinthian discord.

land understood that they had come to spy out their country, and sent men to arrest them, that they might be put to death. But Rahab received them hospitably and concealed them in the upper chamber under the flax-stalks. And when the king's messengers arrived and said, "*The spies of our land entered in unto thee: bring them forth, for so the king commandeth;*" she made answer, "*Yea, the men whom ye seek entered in unto me: but they departed straightway* (cf. Josh. ii. 3—5), and they are journeying on their way," at the same time pointing them in the wrong direction. And she said to the men, "*Of a truth I know that the Lord your God is delivering unto you this country, for the fear and dread of you is fallen upon the inhabitants of it. When therefore it shall be that ye take it, save me and my father's house.*" And they said unto her, "*It shall be as thou hast said unto us. When thou shalt know that we are at hand, thou shalt gather all thy kindred beneath thy roof, and they shall be saved. For any that are found outside the house shall perish*" (Josh. ii. 9, 13, 18, 19). And they went on to give her a sign, which was that she should hang a scarlet thread from her house: in this way they signified beforehand that all who believed and hoped in God would find redemption through the blood of the Lord.[1] Observe, beloved, that the woman possessed not only faith but the gift of prophecy.

XIII. Therefore, brethren, let us put away all haughtiness and pride and foolishness and angry passions, and let us be humble-minded, and let us do as it is written: for the Holy Spirit says, *Let not the wise man glory in his wisdom,*

---

[1] This is the one exception to the rule which governs Clement's use of the Old Testament. Elsewhere it is straightforward, very different from the forced allegorizing of many of the early Christian writers.

neither let the mighty man glory in his might, let not the rich man glory in his riches; but let him that glorieth glory in the Lord, that he may seek Him out, and do judgment and righteousness (1 Sam. ii. 10; Jer. ix. 23, 24). Above all, let us remember the words of the Lord Jesus, when He was teaching forbearance and longsuffering: for He said,[1] *Be merciful, that ye may obtain mercy; forgive, that ye may be forgiven. As ye do, so shall it be done unto you; as ye give, so shall it be given unto you; as ye judge, so shall ye be judged; as ye show kindness, so shall ye receive kindness; with what measure ye mete, it shall be measured unto you* (St. Matt. v. 7; vi. 14; vii. 1, 2; St. Luke vi. 31, 36—38). In this commandment and these ordinances let us establish ourselves, that we may walk obediently to His holy words, in all humility. For the holy word saith, *Unto whom shall I look, but unto the man that is meek and quiet, and that trembleth at my oracles?* (Is. lxvi. 2).

XIV. It is right and incumbent upon us, therefore, my brethren, to obey God rather than follow men who by their presumption and disorderliness have given rise to detestable jealousy. For it is no common damage that we shall incur, but rather serious peril, if we are so foolhardy as to hand ourselves over to the purposes of men who would plunge into strife and divisions, if so they might alienate us from that which is good. Let us be kind to one another,[2] according to the tenderness and sweetness of our Maker. For it is written, *The kind shall inhabit the land, and the blameless shall be left upon it,*

---

[1] A very loose quotation, probably, as in many other cases, from memory.
[2] Another reading which Lightfoot accepts, gives, "Let us be kind to them," *i.e.* the leaders of the division; but this hardly seems to be in accord with the preceding words. The Latin version gives "nobis," as translated above.

but the transgressors shall be utterly destroyed from it (Prov. ii. 21, 22; Ps. xxxvii. 9, 38). And again He saith, *I saw the ungodly exalted above measure, and lifted up like the cedars of Libanus. And I passed by, and lo, he was not, and I sought out his place and I found it not. Keep innocency, and have an eye to integrity, for there is a memorial[1] for the man of peace* (Ps. xxxvii. 35–37).

XV. So then let us cling to those who live in peace with godliness, and not to those who seek for peace with guile. For He saith in a place, *This people honoureth Me with their lips, but their heart is far from Me* (Is. xxix. 13). And again, *With their mouth they were blessing, but in their heart they were cursing* (Ps. lxii. 4). And again He saith, *They loved Him with their mouth, and with their tongue they spake lies unto Him, and their heart was not right with Him, nor were they steadfast in His covenant* (Ps. lxxviii. 36, 37). *Therefore let the crafty lips be put to silence, which speak wickedness against the righteous man* (Ps. xxxi. 18). And again, *May the Lord destroy all the crafty lips, and the haughty tongue, even those who say, Let us magnify our tongue: our lips are our own: who is lord over us? For the oppression of the poor, and for the sighing of the needy, now will I arise, saith the Lord; I will set him in safety, I will deal boldly by him* (Ps. xii. 3—5).

XVI. For the humble-minded it is to whom Christ belongs, and not those who exalt themselves against His flock. Our Lord Jesus Christ, who is the Sceptre of the greatness of God,[2] though He might have come with a display of pride and haughtiness, yet came with humility,[3]

---

[1] A memorial, *i.e.* posterity.
[2] This expression is doubtless suggested by Ps. cx. 2, "The Lord shall send forth the rod of Thy strength."
[3] Cf. Phil. ii. 6—8.

even as the Holy Spirit spake concerning Him; for He saith, *Lord, who believed our report, and to whom was the arm of the Lord revealed? We proclaimed Him before the Lord. He is as a little child,*[1] *as a root in thirsty ground. There is no form nor glory in Him. When we saw Him, He had no form nor beauty, but His form was without honour, lacking more than the form of men. A man smitten and full of toil, and knowing how to endure weakness; for He hath His face turned away from us. He was dishonoured, and was not esteemed. He beareth our sins, and suffereth pangs for our sakes, and we did esteem Him smitten and full of toil and in misery. And He was wounded for our sins, and hath been put to pain for our transgressions. The chastisement of our peace was upon Him; with His stripes we were healed. We all wandered astray like sheep, every man in his own way. And the Lord delivered Him up for our sins, and for His own pains He openeth not His mouth. As a lamb to the slaughter, so was He led, and as a sheep before her shearer is dumb, so He openeth not His mouth. In His humiliation His judgment was taken away. His generation who shall declare? for His life is taken from the earth: for the transgressions of my people He is come unto death. And I will give the wicked for His burial,*[2] *and the rich for His death,*[2] *because He did no transgression, neither was guile found in His mouth: and the Lord seeketh to cleanse Him from His stroke. If ye make an offering for sin, your soul shall see a seed that shall live long. And the Lord seeketh to diminish from the toil of His soul, and to show light unto*

---

[1] "He is as a little child:" this is omitted by the Latin version.
[2] *For* His burial, *for* His death: the word in the Septuagint is ἀντί, which can only mean in requital for. Our text, therefore, cannot be explained as referring to the thieves between whom our Lord was crucified, or to the tomb of Joseph, where He was laid.

Him, and to fill Him[1] *with understanding, to justify a righteous Man that serveth many well; and He shall bear their sins Himself. Therefore He shall inherit many, and shall divide the spoils of the strong, because His soul was delivered up to death, and He was reckoned among the transgressors. And He Himself bare the sins of many, and for their sins was delivered up* (Is. liii.). And again He saith Himself,[2] *But I am a worm and no man, a scorn of men and an outcast of the people. All they that saw Me laughed Me to scorn, they spake with their lips, they shook their head, saying, He hoped in the Lord, let Him deliver him, let Him save him, for He desireth him* (Ps. xxii. 6, 8). See, beloved, what is the pattern that has been given to us: for if the Lord was so humble, what must we do, who through Him passed beneath the yoke of His grace?

XVII. Let us be imitators of those others also, who went about in goat-skins and sheep-skins,[3] preaching the coming of Christ; Elijah, for example, and Elisha, and also Ezekiel; and besides them, those who were approved. Abraham was highly commended, and was called the friend of God;[4] and yet, while he gazed upon the glory of God, he said with all humility, *But I am dust and ashes* (Gen. xviii. 27). Again it is written thus concerning Job, *Now Job was righteous and blameless, speaking truth and fearing God, one that abstained from all evil* (Job i. 1). Yet he accuses himself, and says, *No man is clean from impurity, not though his life be but for a day* (Job

---

[1] Reading πλῆσαι, which is Grabe's conjecture, from comparison with the Hebrew text, instead of πλάσαι. The Latin version, however, reads firmare (formare?).

[2] *i.e.* Christ, who is regarded as the speaker in this Psalm.

[3] A reminiscence of Heb. xi. 37. Elijah's mantle (1 Kings xix. 13; 2 Kings ii. 8) is rendered μηλωτή, sheep-skin, in the Septuagint.

[4] Isaiah xli. 8.

xiv. 4, 5). Moses was called *faithful in all His house*,[1] and through his ministration God judged the Egyptians by their plagues and sufferings. But although he too was greatly glorified, his heart was not lifted up, but, when the answer came to him at the bush, he said, *Who am I, that Thou dost send me? I am slow of speech, and of a slow tongue* (Ex. iii. 11; iv. 10). And again he saith, *But I am smoke from a pot*.[2]

XVIII. But what are we to say of David, who was so highly commended, that God said of him, *I found a man after My heart, David the son of Jesse; with everlasting mercy did I anoint him* (1 Sam. xiii. 14; Ps. lxxxix. 21). Yet he also says unto God, *Have mercy upon me, O God, after Thy great mercy, and according to the multitude of Thy compassions blot out my transgression. Wash me more fully from my transgression and cleanse me from my sin: for I acknowledge my transgression and my sin is ever before me. Against Thee only did I sin, and did that which was evil in Thy sight; that Thou mayest be justified in Thy words and mayest overcome when Thou dost plead.*[3] *For behold in transgressions was I conceived, and in sins did my mother bring me forth. For behold, Thou didst love truth; the dark secrets of Thy wisdom didst Thou show me. Thou shalt sprinkle me with hyssop, and I shall be cleansed; Thou shalt wash me, and I shall be made white above snow. Thou shalt make me to hear of joy and gladness; the bones which have been humbled shall rejoice. Turn away Thy face from my sins, and blot out*

---

[1] "*His* house." The Septuagint has "My," and the Latin version has "domo Dei." Numbers xii. 7.

[2] The source of this quotation is unknown. Lightfoot, in a note on the quotations of Clement from apocryphal sources, suggests that it is drawn from *The Prophesying of Eldad and Medad*, from which a quotation occurs in the Second Vision of Hermas, cp. 3.

[3] For the pleading of God, cf. Isaiah v. 3, "Judge, I pray you, betwixt Me and My vineyard."

all my transgressions. Create a clean heart in me, O God, and renew a right spirit in my inward parts. Cast me not away from Thy presence, and take not Thy Holy Spirit from me. Restore unto me the joy of Thy salvation, and stablish me with a generous[1] *spirit. I will teach Thy ways unto transgressors, and ungodly men shall be converted unto Thee. Deliver me from bloodguiltiness, O God, Thou God of my salvation. My tongue shall rejoice in Thy righteousness. Thou shalt open my mouth, O Lord, and my lips shall show forth Thy praise. For if Thou hadst desired sacrifice, I would have given it; with burnt offerings Thou wilt not be pleased. A sacrifice unto God is a broken spirit; a broken and humble heart God will not despise* (Ps. li. 1–17).

XIX. So then all these great men received commendation, and it is through obedience that their humblemindedness and reverence[2] have made us better as well as the generations before us, even those who received His oracles in fear and truth. Inasmuch therefore as we have participated in all these great and famous doings,[3] let us now return to the goal[4] of peace which has been from the beginning and has been handed down to us; let us fix our gaze on the Father and Creator of the universe, and let us dwell upon His noble and surpassing gifts of peace and deeds of goodwill. Let us behold Him with

[1] The Greek word is ἡγεμονικόν. As a substantive, this word is frequently employed by Origen in a philosophical sense, to express the ruling part of each man's nature; here the word is used adjectivally, and implies "that which befits a ruler," *i. e.* generous.

[2] Lightfoot translates "submissiveness," disagreeing with various lexicographers, who explain ὑποδεὲς by ὑπόφοβον, *i. e.* "fearfulness," or reverence.

[3] Because we have just been considering the examples of Abraham, Job, Moses, and David, and we are the heirs of past ages.

[4] The goal of peace is God: peace comes from Him, and seeks to return to Him, when men imitate His peacefulness.

our mind, and let the eyes of our soul contemplate His long-suffering will. Let us consider how slow to anger He is towards all His Creation.

XX. The heavens obey Him, moving in peace according to His ordinance. Day and night complete the course which He has appointed them, giving no hindrance one to the other. The sun, the moon, and the stars in their twinkling dance, preserve due concord [1] and never swerve aside, while according to His plan they unfold the courses assigned to them. The earth teems with produce at her proper seasons in obedience to His will, and sendeth forth food in abundance for men and beasts and all the living creatures upon her face, without variance and without any change from what He has appointed.

The unfathomable depths of the abysses and the unutterable statutes [2] of the world below are bound by the same ordinances. The hollow of the measureless sea collected by His operation *into its reservoirs* [3] transgresses not the bounds that are set around it, but it does according as He gave it commandment. For He said, *So far shalt thou come, and thy waves shall be broken within thee* (Job xxxviii. 11). The ocean that men cannot pass and the worlds beyond it [4] are governed by the same directions of the Master. The seasons of spring and summer and autumn and winter give place to one

---

[1] Concord is the dominating thought of the Epistle; and especially of this chapter, which is a panegyric of harmony and peace, as displayed in the natural world, according to the Creator's design.

[2] The reading κρίματα (which Lightfoot retained) has received additional confirmation from the Latin version, which reads "judicia."

[3] Gen. i. 9.

[4] It would be absurd to attempt to decide what Clement had in mind when he wrote of the worlds beyond the Ocean, seeing that his idea of the ocean was the same as that of the ancients generally, viz. a river flowing round the earth. Cf. § 33, "He divided the earth from the sea that surrounds it."

another in peace. The weights[1] of the winds accomplish their ministry at their proper times without discord; the perennial fountains, made to give enjoyment and health, offer to men unceasingly their life-giving breasts. The very smallest of living creatures come together in harmony and peace. All these works of His hands the great Creator and Master of the universe ordained should move in peace and harmony, thus conferring benefit upon them all, but especially upon us who have fled for refuge to His compassions through our Lord Jesus Christ, to whom be glory and majesty for ever. Amen.

XXI. Beware, beloved, lest His many benefits become a judgment unto us all, if we live not worthily of Him and do with concord those things which are good and well-pleasing in His sight. For He saith in a certain place, *The Spirit of the Lord is a lamp searching the innermost chambers of the belly* (Prov. xx. 27). Let us see how near He is, and that none of our thoughts or of the disputings in which we engage escapes Him. It is right therefore that we should not be deserters from His will: rather than offend God, let us be willing to give offence to foolish and senseless men, who are uplifted and boastful in the vauntingness of speech. Let us reverence the Lord Jesus Christ, whose blood was given on our behalf.[2] Let us venerate our rulers. Let us do honour to the older men, let us bring up our

---

[1] The weights, σταθμοί. Lightfoot refers to Job xxviii. 25, "To make a weight for the wind" (R.V.), but he thinks that Clement may have misunderstood the meaning of the word, and accordingly translates by "fixed stations," though the proper word for that meaning would be στάσεις. The Latin version translates by "pondera," while the Septuagint gives "pondus."

[2] The Latin version seems at fault here. It spoils the balance of the sentence by translating, "rather than offend God or our Lord Jesus Christ, whose blood was shed on our behalf. Let us reverence our rulers, venerate and do honour to the older men."

young men in the fear of God. Let us direct our women towards that which is good: let them display the lovable disposition of purity, let them manifest their sincere desire after meekness, let them prove their control over their tongue by their silence; let there be no partiality in their regard,[1] but let it be shown equally and with all purity to all who fear God. Let your children be partakers of the education that is in Christ; let them learn how humility avails with God, what power pure love has with God, how the fear of Him is good and great and saves all who walk in it in holiness with a clean heart. For God is a searcher of the thoughts and intents:[2] His breath is in us, and whensoever He will, He shall take it away.

XXII. Now faith in Christ confirms[3] all this; for He Himself through the Holy Spirit calls us in these words: *Come, ye children, hearken unto Me, I will teach you the fear of the Lord. What man is he that seeketh life, and loveth to see good days? Keep thy tongue from evil, and thy lips from speaking guile. Turn from evil and do good; seek peace and pursue it. The eyes of the Lord are over the righteous, and His ears are toward their prayer; but the face of the Lord is against them that do evil, to destroy the remembrance of them from the earth. The righteous cried, and the Lord heard him, and delivered him from all his afflictions. Many are the afflictions of the righteous, and from them all shall the Lord deliver*

---

[1] I translate ἀγάπη as "regard" here, because it is impossible to bring out in English the difference between φιλεῖν and ἀγαπᾶν, if they are both translated by "love." "The disciple whom Jesus loved" is sometimes ὃν ἠγάπα, which implies moral choice; and once ὃν ἐφίλει, which speaks of personal affection. Cf. Westcott *in loc.*

[2] Cf. Heb. iv. 12, "The word of God ... is a discerner of the thoughts and intents of the heart."

[3] Secures, *i. e.* this power of prevailing with God.

him (Ps. xxxiv. 11—17, 19). And again, *Many are the stripes of the sinner, but they that hope in the Lord, mercy shall compass them about* (Ps. xxxii. 10).

XXIII. The all-compassionate and gracious Father is loving to them that fear Him, and bestows His gifts with kindness and affection upon all who come to Him with a sincere heart. Let us therefore not be double-minded, and let not our soul be wayward, when we think of His surpassing and glorious gifts. Far from us be this Scripture,[1] where He saith, *Miserable are the double-minded, who doubt in their soul, who say, We heard these things also in the time of our fathers, and behold, we have grown old, and none of them hath come upon us. Ye fools, compare yourselves to a tree; the vine first sheds its leaves, then it puts forth a shoot, then a leaf, then a flower; afterwards comes the hard berry, and then the ripe grape.* Ye see that it takes a short time for the fruit of the tree to come to maturity. In very truth quickly and suddenly shall His purpose be fulfilled, as the Scripture also bears witness, *He shall come quickly and shall not tarry*, and *Suddenly shall the Lord come into His temple, even the Holy One, whom ye look for* (Hab. ii. 3; Mal. iii. 1).

XXIV. Let us understand, beloved, how the Master is for ever showing us the resurrection that shall be, of which He made the Lord Jesus Christ to be the first-fruits when He raised Him from the dead. Let us mark, beloved, the resurrection which takes place at its proper season. Day and night show us a resurrection: the night is laid to rest, the day arises; the day passes away, and the night ensues. Look at the fruits, consider the manner and method of the sowing. *The sower goes*

---

[1] Lightfoot suggests that this is a quotation from the apocryphal book of *The Prophesying of Eldad and Medad.*

forth (St. Matt. xiii. 3), and casts each of the seeds upon the earth; and they fall dry and bare [1] and bury themselves in the earth and decay. Then out of their decay the Master in His mighty providence raises them up, and out of one many make increase and bring forth fruit.

XXV. Let us not forget that remarkable sign, which appears in the East, that is, in the parts about Arabia. There is a bird called the phœnix.[2] It is for ever alone of its kind, and lives five hundred years. And when the hour of its dissolution is at hand, it makes for itself a coffin of frankincense and myrrh and the other spices, and, when the time is fulfilled, it enters into it and dies. And as its flesh decays, a worm comes into being which draws its nourishment from the moisture of the dead creature and puts forth wings. Then, when it has attained strength, it takes the coffin in which are the bones of the dead, and makes its way with them from the land of Arabia to the Egyptian city called Heliopolis.[3] There in full day and in the sight of all, it flies to the altar of the Sun and lays them upon it, and then returns. The priests, in consequence, inspect the records of the times, and find that the phœnix has arrived on the completion of the five hundredth year.

XXVI. Do we then think it a great or wonderful thing that the Creator of all will raise up all who have served Him in holiness and in the confidence of a good

---

[1] Cf. 1 Cor. xv. 37, "Thou sowest not that body that shall be, but bare grain."

[2] Clement is not more credulous than the heathen writers of his own generation, of whom Tacitus serves as a good example. In the *Annals*, Bk. VI, he devotes a chapter to the discussion of the reported reappearance of the phœnix in Egypt. His tone is slightly sceptical, but he does not attempt to deny the existence of such a bird as the phœnix.

[3] *i.e.* the City of the Sun.

faith, seeing that even a bird is made to show the mightiness of His promise? For He saith in a certain place, *And Thou shalt raise me up, and I will make confession unto Thy name* (Ps. xxviii. 7?). And, *I laid me down and slept; I awoke, for Thou art with me* (Ps. iii. 5). And again Job says, *And Thou shalt raise up this my body that hath suffered all these pains* (Job xix. 26, Septuagint).

XXVII. Let this hope then serve to bind fast our souls to God, for He is faithful in His promises and just in His judgments. He who gave commandment not to lie, will much less lie himself; for to lie is the one thing which is impossible with God. Therefore let our faith in Him burn more brightly within us,[1] and let us understand that all things stand near to Him. By the word of His majesty He framed the universe, and by that word He can overthrow it. *Who shall say unto Him, what hast Thou done? or who shall withstand the might of His strength?* (Wisdom xii. 12). He will do all things as He chooses and when He chooses, and none of the things that He has decreed shall fail. All things are in His sight, and nothing is hidden from His counsel, seeing that *the heavens declare the glory of God, and the firmament telleth forth the work of His hands. Day unto day uttereth speech, and night unto night telleth forth knowledge; and there are no words nor voices, whose sounds are not heard* (Ps. xix. 1—3).

XXVIII. Inasmuch then as He sees and hears all things, let us fear Him, and let us cease from shameful lustings after evil works, in order that we may find shelter

---

[1] Lightfoot here renders ἡ πίστις αὐτοῦ by "His faithfulness," as in Romans iii. 3; but the argument is—"Inasmuch as we possess all the preceding testimonies to a future resurrection, let us hope, and let us trust in Him more firmly." For πίστις with gen. cf. Acts iii. 16, τῇ πίστει τοῦ ὀνόματος αὐτοῦ.

beneath His mercy from the judgments to come. For where can any of us escape from His mighty hand? And where is the world that will receive any of those who desert from His service? For the writing[1] saith in a certain place, *Where shall I go and where shall I hide from Thy face? If I mount up to heaven, Thou are there; if I depart into the extremities of the earth, there is Thy right hand; if I make my bed in the abysses,[2] there is Thy Spirit* (Ps. cxxxix. 7, 8). Whither then shall a man go, or where shall he escape from God, seeing that He embraceth the world?

XXIX. Let us approach Him therefore in holiness of soul, lifting to Him hands holy and undefiled, loving our gentle and tender Father, who elected us unto Himself as His own portion.[3] For thus it is written, *When the Most High was dividing the nations, when He separated the children of Adam, He set the bounds of the nations according to the number of the angels of God.*[4] *His people Jacob was made the portion of the Lord, and Israel the lot of His inheritance* (Deut. xxxii. 8, 9), and in another place He saith, *Behold, the Lord taketh for Himself a nation*

---

[1] γραφεῖον. "The law, the prophecies, and the rest of the books" form a three-fold division of the Old Testament referred to in the Prologue to Ecclesiasticus; this same division occurs in St. Luke xxiv. 44, where we read, "The law of Moses, the Prophets, and the Psalms." τὰ γραφεῖα was the technical name for the third division, and properly speaking included the Psalms, from which this quotation is taken.

[2] In Hell (A.V.) ἡ ἄβυσσος is the word translated "the deep" in St. Luke viii. 31. In Rev. xx. 1 (and everywhere in Rev.) it is translated, "the bottomless pit."

[3] μέρος ἐκλογῆς, lit. a portion of election, *i. e.* an elect portion; cf. Acts ix. 15, σκεῦος ἐκλογῆς, lit. a vessel of election, *i. e.* an elect vessel.

[4] This is the reading of the Septuagint, and is adopted by Clement. The meaning is that while the angels were set in charge of the nations, Israel was the special care of God. The Christian Church, as being the spiritual Israel, has now entered this place of privilege.

out of the midst of the nations, as a man taketh the first-fruits of his threshing-floor, and there shall come forth from that nation the holy of holies (Deut iv. 34; xiv. 2; Numb. xviii. 27; 2 Chr. xxxi. 14; Ezek. xlviii. 12).

XXX. Inasmuch then as we are the portion of a Holy One, let us do all those things that belong to holiness. Let us flee from evil-speakings, shameful and unclean intimacies, drunkennesses and factions and hateful lusts, vile adultery, hateful pride. *For God*, saith He, *resisteth the proud, but giveth grace unto the humble* (James iv. 6). Let us therefore be among those to whom this grace hath been given from God; let us put on the garment of concord, let us be humble-minded and temperate, let us shun all whispering and evil-speaking, let us be justified not by our words, but by our works. For He saith, *The man of many words shall not be unanswered; and doth the man full of speech think to be justified?* (Job xi. 2). *Blessed is the man that is born of a woman and liveth but a few days.*[1] *Let thy words be few* (Job xi. 3). Let our praise be in God, and let it not come from ourselves, for they that praise themselves are an abomination unto God. Let the testimony to our well-doing come from others, even as it was borne unto our fathers for their righteousness. Leave boldness and insolence and recklessness to them that are under the curse of God; but reasonableness[2] and lowliness and meekness should be found among those whom God has blessed.

---

[1] This sentence, "Blessed...few days" has obviously no connection with the context. Lightfoot suggests that it has crept in by an error in the transcription from the original, whereby words from Job xiv. 1 in a parallel column, were incorporated with this passage.

[2] ἐπιείκεια. Here we are introduced to another dominating word of the Epistle. Concord has been impressed upon the Corinthians, now they are encouraged to display reasonableness.

XXXI. Let us hold fast then to His blessing, and let us mark what are the ways of blessing. Let us open the records at the very beginning. Why was Abraham our father blessed? Was it not because he wrought righteousness and truth through faith? Isaac, though he knew for a surety the death that lay before him, nevertheless was led cheerfully as a sacrifice. Jacob with all humility departed from his land because of his brother, and journeyed unto Laban, and served him; and the twelve tribes of Israel were given unto him.

XXXII. If a man will consider them severally and with sincerity, he will come to learn the splendour of the gifts that He has given. For from Jacob spring all the priests and Levites who serve the altar of God: of him is the Lord Jesus as concerning the flesh; of him, in the line of Judah, are kings and governors and rulers; while the rest of his tribes stand in no small honour, according to the promise of God, *Thy seed shall be as the stars of heaven* (Gen. xv. 5).

Not one of these was glorified or magnified through themselves or their works or the righteousness which they displayed, but only through the will of God. In like manner we, being called in Christ-Jesus by His will, are not justified through ourselves or our wisdom or our understanding or our piety or the works that we have done in holiness of heart, <u>but by faith</u>, by which Almighty God justified all men that have been from the beginning: to Whom be glory for ever and ever. Amen.

XXXIII. What then must we do, brethren? Must we be idle in well-doing? Must we cease from love? The Master forbid that this should be so with *us*, but let us endeavour with fervent zeal to accomplish every good work.[1]

---

[1] § 32 has shown the vital necessity of faith. In order to preserve

The Creator and Master of the world Himself rejoices in His works. For by the vastness of His power He established the heavens, and by His incomprehensible understanding He disposed them. And the earth He divided from the sea that surrounds it, and fixed it on the secure foundation of His own will; and the living creatures that move thereon He commanded to exist by His decree: and the sea and the living creatures that are in it which He had created before them, He enclosed by His power. Above all these—supreme and most marvellous to conceive[1] of! with His sacred and faultless hands He moulded man after the fashion of His own image. For thus saith God: *Let us make man after our image and after our likeness. And God made man; male and female made He them* (Gen. i. 26, 27). When, therefore, He had completed all these things, He pronounced them good, and blessed them, and said, *Be fruitful and multiply* (Gen. i. 28).

We saw before that good works were the adornment of all the righteous: now we see that the Lord Himself rejoiced in adorning Himself with His works.

With this example before our eyes, let us not be slow to meet His will, but let us work the work of righteousness with all our strength.

XXXIV. The good workman receives the bread of his work with confidence, but the sluggish and remiss workman will not face his employer. We must, therefore, be earnest in well-doing, for of God are all things. For He tells us before, saying, *Behold, the Lord, and His reward*

---

the balance of doctrine, Clement hastens to show that good works are none the less necessary.

[1] κατὰ διάνοιαν. These words are not represented in the Latin version, but the same expression occurs in chap. xix. where it is translated "sensu nostro." That is probably the meaning here.

is before His face, to render unto every man according to his work (Is. xl. 10; lxii. 11; Prov. xxiv. 12). He counsels us therefore to believe on Him [1] with all our heart, and not to be idle or remiss in any good work. Let our boasting and our confidence be in Him; let us submit to His will; let us observe how His will is ministered to by the entire host of His angels which stands before Him. For the Scripture saith, *Ten thousand times ten thousand stood before Him, and thousand thousands ministered unto Him, and they cried, Holy, Holy, Holy, Lord of Hosts, all the creation is full of His glory* (Dan. vii. 10; Is. vi. 3). Let us also meet together, therefore, with our inmost hearts in concord,[2] and with fervour let us cry unto Him as with one mouth, that we may be made partakers in His great and glorious promises. For He saith, *Eye hath not seen, nor ear heard, neither hath it entered into the heart of man how great things He hath prepared for them that wait for Him.*[3]

XXXV. How gracious and admirable are the gifts of God, beloved! Life in immortality, activity in righteousness, truth in confidence, faith in assurance, temperateness in sanctification! And if all these are now within our apprehension, what must be the things that are being prepared for *them that wait for Him?* The Creator and Father of the ages in His perfect holiness alone knows

---

[1] ἐπ' αὐτῷ. Lightfoot renders this in his note on the passage, "with our reward in view." But the change would be too violent to ἐν αὐτῷ in the next sentence, which must be rendered "in Him."

[2] In concord. This chapter has a liturgical character, and the thought of concord belongs both to the Epistle as a whole, and to the liturgical tone of the passage.

[3] There has been much discussion as to the source of this quotation. It is more probable that it is a reminiscence of 1 Cor. ii. 9, which in turn seems to be drawn from Is. lxiv. 4, than that it is a quotation, on the part of both Clement and Paul, from a lost apocryphal work, as is suggested by Origen.

their magnitude and their splendour. Let us then endeavour earnestly to be found in the number of those who wait for Him, that we may be partakers of His promised gifts. And how shall this be, beloved? Only if our mind be stablished by faith toward God; only if we seek out the things which are well pleasing and acceptable unto Him ; only if we accomplish the things that agree with His stainless will and we follow the way of truth, by casting off all unrighteousness and transgression, covetousness, strifes, malicious and crafty tempers, whisperings and evil-speakings, defiance of God, haughtiness and insolence, vainglory and inhospitality. For they that practise these things are an abomination to God ; and not only they, but all who take pleasure in them that practise them.[1] For the Scripture saith, *But unto the sinner said God, Why dost thou declare My statutes, and takest My covenant in thy mouth? But thou didst hate instruction and wast casting My words behind thee. If thou sawest a thief, thou consentedst with him, and with the adulterers thou didst set thy lot. Thy mouth increased wickedness, and thy tongue wove deceitfulness. Thou didst sit and speak evil against thy brother, and thou didst lay a stumbling-block in the way of thy mother's son. These things thou didst and I kept silence; thou thoughtest, thou transgressor, that I should be like unto thyself; but I will convict thee and show thee to thyself. Therefore understand this, ye that forget God, lest at any time He seize you like a lion and there be none to deliver. The sacrifice of praise shall glorify Me, and therein is the way whereby I will show him the salvation of God* (Ps. l. 16--23).

---

[1] This is a reminiscence of Romans i. 32, "Who, knowing ... that they which commit such things are worthy of death, not only do the same, but have pleasure in them that do them."

XXXVI. This is the way, beloved, which led us to our salvation, Jesus Christ, the High Priest of our offerings, our Guardian and Helper in our weakness. Through Him let us gaze into the heavenly heights; through Him we behold as in a mirror [1] His flawless and transcendent visage. Through Him the eyes of our heart were opened; through Him our mind, once foolish and hidden in darkness, shoots up unto the light; through Him the Master willed that we should taste of the immortal knowledge; through Him, *who, being the effulgence of His majesty, is by so much greater than angels, as He hath inherited a more excellent name than they* (Heb. i. 3, 4). For it is written thus, *Who maketh His angels spirits and His ministers a flame of fire* (Ps. civ. 4): but concerning His Son thus spake the Master, *Thou art My Son, I have begotten Thee this day. Ask of Me, and I will give Thee nations for Thine inheritance, and the ends of the earth for Thy possession* (Ps. ii. 7, 8). And again He saith unto Him, *Sit on My right hand, until I make Thine enemies Thy footstool* (Ps. cx. 1). Who then are His enemies? Who but the wicked and they that resist His will?

XXXVII. Let us serve therefore, brethren, with all determination under His faultless commands. Let us take a lesson from the soldiers who serve under our rulers, and let us mark the order, the promptitude,[2] the submissiveness with which they execute the orders they receive. They are not all prefects, or rulers of thousands, or rulers of hundreds, or rulers of fifties, and so on; but

---

[1] Or, reflect as a mirror. Cf. the alternative translation of κατοπτρίζεσθαι in R.V. 2 Cor. iii. 18, "reflecting as a mirror," and (*marg.*) "beholding as in a mirror." The Latin version gives "tamquam per speculum uidemus."

[2] Reading ἐκτικῶς with C.

every man in his own rank executes the orders he receives from the emperor or his superiors. The great cannot exist without the small, nor the small without the great. There is a kind of connection between all things, and herein lies their serviceableness. To take our body as an example : the head without the feet is nothing, even as the feet without the head are nothing; in truth the smallest members of our body are necessary and useful to the whole body. But all the members agree in submitting to one authority, that the soundness of the whole may be preserved.[1]

XXXVIII. In our case then let the whole body be kept sound in Christ Jesus, and let each man submit himself to his neighbour, according as he was appointed by the special gift that God gave him.[2] The strong must not neglect the weak, and the weak must respect the strong. The rich should furnish help[3] unto the poor, while the poor should thank God for the gift of one by whom his wants may be supplied. Let the wise man display his wisdom by good works and not merely by subtlety of words :[4] let the lowly man not bear testimony

---

[1] This analogy is drawn from St. Paul's exhortation to unity in 1 Cor. xii.

[2] χάρισμα. This word is regularly translated gift in the New Testament, cf. 1 Peter iv. 10, "As every man hath received the *gift.*" χαρίσματα, gifts, are different aspects of the χάρις, free bounty, of God. χαρίσματα are "free gifts from the Lord of men, . . . designed by Him to be distinctive qualifications for rendering distinctive services to men or to communities of men." Hort, *Ecclesia,* p. 154.

[3] ἐπιχορηγείτω. Cf. Gal. iii. 5 (R.V.), "He that supplieth to you the Spirit." There is an idea of liberality in this word, denoting originally, as it does, an office in the Greek state devolving only on a rich man.

[4] σοφὸς, σοφίαν. The word σοφία occurs no less than fifteen times in the first two chapters of 1 Cor., and, like γνῶσις, seems to have been a possession on which the Corinthians prided themselves unduly. μὴ ἐν λόγοις, cf. 1 Cor. i. 17, "not with wisdom of

to himself, but let him leave his lowliness to receive testimony from another. If a man has kept his body in chastity, let him be chaste; yet let him not boast, for he must know that it is Another and not himself that furnishes unto him his gift of continence. Let us therefore consider, brethren, the matter of which we were made; who and what we were when we came into the world; let us consider the sepulchral darkness from which our Fashioner and Creator brought us into His world, where His benefits awaited us, before ever we were born. Seeing then that we have all these bounties from His hand, we are bound in all things to give Him thanks. To Him be glory for ever and ever. Amen.

XXXIX. Foolish and thoughtless and absurd and ignorant men mock at us and revile us, because they desire to be exalted in their own hearts. But what can mortal man do? What strength has a man that is dust? For it is written, *There was no form before my eyes: only I heard a breath and a voice. What! shall mortal man be clean before the Lord, or shall a man find no reproof for his works? For against His servants He is distrustful, and against His angels He taketh note of some waywardness. Yea, the heaven is not clean in His sight. Let alone them that dwell in houses of clay, whereof we ourselves are made, even of the selfsame clay. He smiteth them like a moth, and betwixt morning and evening they are no more. Because they could not succour themselves, they perished; He breathed upon them and they died, because they had no wisdom. But call, if any shall heed thee, or if thou shalt see one of the holy angels. For in truth wrath*[1] *killeth a foolish man, and jealousy slayeth*

---

words," and 1 Cor. ii. 4, "not with enticing words of man's wisdom."

[1] Wrath against God.

him that is gone astray. I have seen the foolish putting out roots, but straightway their abode was eaten up. Far be their sons from safety: may they be mocked at in the gates of mean men, and there shall not be any to deliver them. For the things which have been laid up by them, the righteous shall eat; but from evils they themselves shall not escape (Job iv. 16—18; xv. 15; iv. 19—v. 5).

XL. Seeing then that these things are plain, and that we have looked into the depths of the Divine knowledge,[1] we are bound to do in due order all those things that the Master commanded us to accomplish at their appointed times. In respect of the offerings and ministrations, not only did He ordain that they should be performed[2] at their appointed times and seasons; but also by His supreme will He Himself set forth the place and the ministers for their performance, that so all things might be done in holiness according to His pleasure and might be acceptable to His will.[3] As many therefore as make their offerings at the appointed seasons are acceptable and blessed, for by following the ordinances of the Master, they are preserved from error. For the high priest is called to perform special ministrations, and the office to which the priests are appointed is special, and upon the Levites special services are laid, and the layman is bound by special ordinances.

[1] Cf. 1 Cor. ii. 10, "The *deep things* of God." Rev. ii. 24, "Have not known the *depths* of Satan." In each case the Greek is τὰ βάθη, as here. To have an inner knowledge of the "depths" of God was one of the Gnostic claims.

[2] The Latin version corroborates S in omitting ἐπιτελεῖσθαι καί, which has crept in from below, and thus renders Lightfoot's addition unnecessary.

[3] Cf. Leviticus vi., where the law of the burnt offering is laid down. This offering was repeated at regular intervals, and with fixed observances.

XLI. Let each of you, brethren, in his own order,[1] give thanks [2] unto God, preserving a good conscience, and adhering to the appointed rule of his service [3] with all reverence. Not in every place, brethren, but only in Jerusalem are the daily sacrifices [4] offered, or the free-will offerings, or the sin offerings and trespass offerings. And even there the offering is made in only one place, in the court of the altar before the sanctuary; and that, not until the offering has been inspected [5] by the high priest and the ministers aforesaid. All who make an offering contrary to the seemly appointment of His will are liable to be punished with death.[6] Yet see, brethren, that

[1] This reference to "order" shows that the rules of the Eucharistic service had been broken. Certain factious persons had induced a number of members of the Corinthian Church to separate themselves from, or endeavour to oppose, their lawfully appointed presbyters, whose duty it was to preside over the offerings. This secession had doubtless been followed by irregular Eucharistic gatherings, where schismatic or self-constituted presbyters had presided. It is in view of this disorder that the duty of ὁμόνοια (concord) is so frequently referred to.
[2] Give thanks, lit. perform his act of *Eucharistia*, or thanksgiving.
[3] Lit. his *liturgia*. λειτουργία was originally a state-duty falling on the richest Athenian citizens, such as providing the cost of a chorus in the theatre (cf. § 38), or fitting out a trireme. In the Septuagint the word is regularly used for the "service" of the priests. In the New Testament it is used of service both to God and man, cf. Phil. ii. 30, "Your lack of service toward me." Later, it was used to denote stated services of the Church, but particularly the Eucharist.
[4] The daily sacrifices, lit. "sacrifices of continuance." This expression occurs in the Septuagint translation of Ex. xxix. 42, and refers to the regular daily sacrifices in the morning and evening. The free-will offerings, lit. "the sacrifices of vows," and the thanksgiving offerings (not mentioned by Clement), were the two classes of peace offerings, provided for in Lev. vii. 11—21. The sin offering and the trespass offering were two classes of expiatory sacrifice, provided for in Lev. iv.-vii. 10. Thus there were three distinct types of sacrifice, the continual burnt offering, the peace offering, the sin offering.
[5] Lit. inspected for blemishes.
[6] Thus Clement shows the importance of order. Three things must be attended to in a sacrifice; the place where the offering is

according as we have been counted worthy to receive fuller knowledge, so is the danger greater to which we are exposed.

XLII. The Apostles were taught the Gospel for our sakes at the feet of the Lord Jesus Christ; Jesus Christ was sent out from God. Christ then is from God, and the Apostles from Christ. Both therefore issued from the will of God with due order. Having therefore received His instructions,[1] and being finally stablished through the Resurrection of our Lord Jesus Christ, and being confident in the word of God they went forth with full conviction from the Holy Spirit,[2] and preached that the Kingdom of God was soon to come. And so, as they preached in the country and in the towns, they proved by the Spirit the first-fruits of their work in each place, and appointed them to be overseers and deacons[3] among them that should believe. And this was no innovation, for from of old it had been written concerning bishops and deacons, as the Scripture says in a certain place, *I will set up their bishops in righteousness, and their deacons in faith.*[4]

XLIII. And is it strange that men who had been divinely charged in Christ with so great a task, should

---

made, the person of the offerer, and the propriety of the thing offered.

[1] Cf. Matt. xxviii. 19, 20; Acts i. 3.
[2] This is a reminiscence of 1 Thess. i. 5.
[3] Not "bishop" in our sense of the word. The word *episcopus* originally implies "function" not "order": thus *episcopi* and *diaconi* (here and in Phil. i. 1) would mean lit. "they that have oversight and they that do service." In this way *episcopi* and *presbyteri* would be the same, the duty of "oversight" being one of the functions of a *presbyterus*. In this Epistle *episcopus* and *presbyterus* and ἡγούμενος (ruler) are convertible terms. *Episcopi* and *diaconi* are coupled together three times, while *episcopus* does not appear in the singular. A threefold ministry, therefore, existed in the lifetime of the Apostles, viz. *apostoli, episcopi* or *presbyteri,* and *diaconi*.
[4] A misquotation from Is. lx. 17.

have appointed these officers? For even the blessed Moses, who was *a faithful servant in all His house*, recorded for a sign in the sacred books all the commands that he had given ; and he was followed by the rest of the prophets, who joined with him in bearing witness to the ordinances he had laid down.[1] For when jealousy arose concerning the priesthood, and there was a division among the tribes as to which of them had been adorned with the glorious office, Moses commanded the twelve princes to bring to him rods, inscribed with the name of each tribe. And he took the rods and bound them and sealed them with the rings of the princes, and laid them up in the tabernacle of the testimony on the table of God. And he shut the tabernacle, and sealed the keys as he had sealed the rods.[2] And he said unto them, "Men and brethren, which tribe soever it be whose rod shall bud, this hath God elected to be priests and ministers unto Him." And when it was day, he gathered all Israel together, six hundred thousand men, and he showed the seals to the princes, and opened the tabernacle of the testimony and took out the rods. And it was found that the rod of Aaron had not only budded, but was bearing fruit.

What think ye, beloved? Did not Moses know before that this would be? Assuredly ; but in order to prevent confusion in Israel, he acted thus that the Name of the only true God might be glorified. To whom be glory for ever and ever. Amen.

[1] This has a general reference. The Apostles surely did right in securing a definite order and due succession, if Moses, who was of all men most faithful, was so careful to render the Law he had given imperishable, and was by Divine appointment followed by the long succession of prophets, who bore witness to the same Law.
[2] S reads "as he had sealed the doors," and Lightfoot accepts this reading, as against A and C, which are now confirmed by the Latin version, in reading "rods." The sealing of the rods and the keys does not form part of the narrative as given in Numbers xvii.

XLIV. No less did our Apostles know through our Lord Jesus Christ that there would be strife over the dignity of the overseer's[1] office. For this very reason, having received complete foreknowledge, they appointed the aforesaid overseers and deacons,[2] and ordained[3] that at their[4] death their ministry should pass into the hands of other[5] tried men. We hold therefore that it is an act of injustice to thrust out from their ministry men who, with the good-will of the entire Church, received their position at the hands of Apostles, or of other honoured men at a later time, and who in all humility ministered

---

[1] Cf. note on cp. 42. This means, obviously, "the office of the *presbyter*."

[2] Cp. 42.

[3] Ordained. All the MS. authorities are at variance here, but the new version offers great help. It will be worth while to examine the evidence, for this is a very good example of textual difficulty. A gives ἐπινομήν, C gives ἐπιδομήν, S gives "superprobatione" (ἐπὶ δοκιμῇ or δοκιμὴν) "dederunt," L gives "legem dederunt." Now, unless the translator of L is in a difficulty, and has attempted to escape from it by translating some unknown word ἐπινομὴ or ἐπιδομὴ (which has been the despair of every commentator) by a safe word such as "legem," the explanation may be perhaps this. A, C, and S spring from a common source (a), perhaps a copy only twice removed from the original, L from a different copy (b). The original text, I suggest, was μεταξὺ νόμον δεδώκασιν. In the margin of the MS. from which (a) sprang was written ἐπὶ δοκιμῇ, referring to δοκιμάσαντες in cp. 42, and to δεδοκιμασμένοι in the succeeding line. When the MS. which produced (a) was copied, these words came into the text, and through a confusion of sound the text stood ΕΠΙΔΟΚΙΜΗΝΟΜΗΝ. Thus we can see how ἐπινομὴν of A and ἐπιδομὴν of C arose, while the translator of S would not understand ΝΟΜΗΝ, and would think it merely an accidental repetition of ΔΟΚΙΜΗΝ. On the other hand L would translate the correct νόμον δεδώκασιν into "legem dederunt," as we find in the Latin version. I am much inclined to trust L here, as in five other places in this chapter alone it proves an invaluable commentary upon difficulties either of text or interpretation.

[4] *i. e.* at the death of the first presbyters appointed by the Apostles, as "si dormierint" in the Latin version shows.

[5] ἕτεροι, *i. e.* a new class of men, appointed by those whom the Apostles had ordained.

to the flock of Christ without offence, peaceably and without presumption, and who have on many occasions been well reported of by all. For we shall be guilty of no small sin, if we reject men who have holily and without offence offered the gifts [1] pertaining to the bishop's office.[2] Blessed are the elders [3] who have departed hence in time past, for they continued till their time was fulfilled and their work had borne fruit ; they have no fear of being removed from their appointed place. We must needs beware ; [4] for ye have taken upon you to put some men out of their office, although they walk discreetly and have held [5] their position without offence.

XLV. Be contentious, brethren, be jealous concerning the things that belong unto salvation. Ye have examined the Holy Scriptures ; they are true, they were given through the Holy Spirit : ye know that in them there is written nothing that is unrighteous or false. Ye

---

[1] "What does Clement mean by *sacrifices*, by *gifts*, and *offerings* ? In what sense are the presbyters said to have presented or offered the gifts ? . . . The sacrifices, offerings, and gifts . . . are the prayers and thanksgivings, the alms, the Eucharistic elements, the contributions to the *agape*, and so forth. . . . The presbyters . . . led the prayers and thanksgivings of the congregation, they presented the alms and contributions to God and asked His blessing on them in the name of the whole body " (Lightfoot).

[2] The Latin version is quite clear on this disputed point, and gives " qui obtulerunt munera episcopatus."

[3] Elders. πρεσβύτεροι. I do not translate this "presbyters" for three reasons : (1) the office has in the preceding sentence been referred to as ἐπισκοπή ; (2) the word bears the same meaning as it does in Heb. xi. 2—" By (faith) the *elders* obtained a good report," *i. e.* the heroes of faith of earlier ages. The "elders" referred to in this passage would be those whose names have been honoured in the earlier chapters of the Epistle ; (3) the Latin version translates *seniores*, which has no reference to ecclesiastical order.

[4] ὁρῶμεν ὅτι. The Latin version renders "videamus quia ; " the subjunctive compels us to translate in the same way as ὁρᾶτε (videte), in § 21.

[5] τετιμημένης. Latin version has "functo."

will not find in them that righteous men have been removed from the company of the holy. Righteous men were persecuted, but it was by the wicked; they were cast into prison, but it was by the unholy; they were stoned, but it was by the disobedient; they were put to death, but by men under the influence of an abominable and unrighteous jealousy. They endured their sufferings nobly. What are we to say, brethren? Was Daniel cast into the den of lions by men that feared God? Were Ananias and Azarias and Misael shut up in the fiery furnace by men devoted to the all-glorious worship of the Most High? God forbid! Who then were the perpetrators of these crimes? Men reprobate and full of all malice, whose heart was so filled with strife and anger that they heaped their cruelties upon those who were serving God with holy and blameless purpose. For they knew not that the Most High champions and defends all who serve His excellent Name with pure conscience; to Whom be glory for ever and ever, Amen. But those who endured with confidence inherited glory and honour, and were exalted, and their names were written by God for a memorial of them for ever and ever. Amen.

XLVI. And so, brethren, we also should hold fast to examples such as these. For it is written, "*Hold fast to the holy,*[1] *for they that hold fast unto them shall be made holy.*" And again in another place He saith, "*With a pure man thou shalt be pure, and with an elect man thou shalt be elect, and with a perverse man thou shalt deal perversely.*"[2] Let us therefore hold fast to such as are pure and righteous: these are the elect of God.

---

[1] The source of this quotation is not known.
[2] In the original quotation, Ps. xviii. 26, 27, "thou" has reference to God: its application here is quite contrary to the sense of the original passage.

Why then are there strifes and angers and parties and divisions and wars among you? Have we not one God and one Christ? Was not one Spirit shed forth upon us? Have we not one calling in Christ?

Why do we rend and tear asunder the members of Christ, and are divided against our own body? Why have we reached such a pitch of madness that we forget that we are members one of another? Remember the words of Jesus our Lord: for He said,[1] "*Woe unto that man: it were good for him if he had not been born, rather than that he should offend one of My elect. It were better for him that a mill-stone should be hanged about him and that he should be drowned in the sea, than that he should pervert one of My elect.*" Many have been perverted by your division; many have been cast into despair, many into doubt, all into sorrow: and yet your dispute continues.

XLVII. Take up the Epistle of the blessed Paul the Apostle. What was the first thing[2] he wrote to you in the beginning[3] of the Gospel? In very truth he admonished you by the Spirit concerning himself and Cephas and Apollos,[4] because even then ye had given way to party-spirit. But the partiality of those days did not involve you in so great a sin as now, for then ye were partisans of Apostles of renown and of a man well-tried in their sight. But now, take heed who they are that have perverted you and have brought disgrace on the glorious

---

[1] This quotation is a combination of two passages, each of which is given in varying form by the three synoptists. Clement is probably quoting from memory (St. Matt. xxvi. 24, and xviii. 6; St. Mark xiv. 21, and ix. 42; St. Luke xxii. 22, and xvii. 1, 2).

[2] τί πρῶτον AC. The Latin version has "quemadmodum," which indicates a Greek reading, τίνα τρόπον, "How did he write?"

[3] The first Epistle to the Corinthians was written probably in A.D. 57, which date would be for the Church at Corinth the early days (or the beginning) of the Gospel.

[4] Cf. Cor. i. 10—13.

name which your love of the brethren [1] had everywhere won for itself. It is shameful, beloved, very shameful—nay more, it is unworthy of your education in Christ, that it should be reported that the Church of Corinth, so long [2] and firmly established as it is, should be divided against its presbyters at the bidding of one or two ringleaders. Nor has this report come only to us: it has reached even those who hold not with us, so that ye cover the name of the Lord with blasphemies because of your folly, and are laying up danger for yourselves besides.

XLVIII. Let us put this sin from us with all speed, and let us fall at the Master's feet and beseech Him with tears to be propitious and to be reconciled to us, and to restore us to that grave and pure manner of living wherein we love the brethren. For love of the brethren is a gate of righteousness that stands open and leads to life, as it is written: "*Open me the gates of righteousness, that I may enter in by them and bless the Lord. This is the gate of the Lord; the righteous shall enter in by it*" (Ps. cxviii. 19, 20). Now there are many gates that stand open, but this is the gate of righteousness, even that which is in Christ, and blessed are they that have entered in thereby and direct their path in holiness and righteousness, doing all things without confusion. If a man be faithful, if he have power to explain a hard saying,[3] if he be wise in

---

[1] In old days the Church of Corinth had been famed for its hospitality, cf. § 1.

[2] So long established, ἀρχαία. If A.D. 57 could be called the beginning of the Gospel for the Corinthians (cf. p. 63), it would be a misuse of words for any one writing much earlier than A.D. 95 to call this Church ἀρχαία. Thus this expression tells against an early date for the Epistle.

[3] A hard saying, γνῶσις. Cf. 1 Cor. xii. 8, "To another the word of 'knowledge'" (γνῶσις). The Gnostics laid claim to an esoteric *gnosis*, which enabled them to penetrate further than others into the depths of God and of the Scriptures. Clement in this passage exhorts the possessor of *gnosis* to be humble, for, as St. Paul said,

discerning words, if he be chaste in his deeds,[1] so much the more humble ought he to be, as he seems to be greater; so much the more ought he to seek the common good of all and not his own.

XLIX. If a man has love in Christ, let him obey the commands of Christ. Who can show forth the bond of the love of God? The splendour of its beauty who can utter? The height to which love uplifts cannot be expressed. Love attaches us to God; "*love covers a multitude of sins*" (1 Pet. iv. 8); love endures all things, is long-suffering in all things. There is nothing assuming, nothing insolent in love. Love[2] has no parties, love does not set men at variance, love does all things in a spirit of peaceableness. In love all the elect of God were made perfect;[3] without love nothing can please God. In love the Master took us to Himself; for the love which He had toward us, Jesus Christ our Lord by the will of God gave His blood for us and His flesh for our flesh and His life for our lives.

L. Ye see, beloved, how great and admirable a thing is love, and how words cannot tell its perfectness. Who is sufficient to be found in love, except those whom God has made worthy? Let us therefore earnestly entreat of His mercy, that we may be found blameless in love, free

---

"*gnosis* puffeth up." This word γνῶσις occurs no less than ten times in 1 Cor.

[1] Lightfoot, following a quotation of this passage made by Clement of Alexandria, introduces γοργὸς, and displaces ἁγνὸς, translating as follows—"let him be strenuous in deeds, let him be pure." But this change was made in face of the evidence of all the MSS. and is further condemned by the Latin version, which keeps the reading of A, C, and S.

[2] Love is the remedy for Corinthian troubles. It knows no *schisma*, no *stasis* (faction); it does everything with concord (one of the leading thoughts of the Epistle).

[3] Cf. 1 John iv. 18.

from that spirit of dissension which is so common.[1] All the generations from Adam unto this day have passed away, but all who by the grace of God were made perfect in love dwell in the place of the godly, and shall be made manifest in the visitation of the Kingdom of God.[2] For it is written,[3] "*Enter into the inner chamber*[4] *for a little while, until Mine anger and wrath have passed away; and I will remember a good day, and will raise you up out of your tombs.*" Hereafter we shall know, beloved, how blessed we are,[5] if we obey the commands of God in concord and love, so that through the love of God our sins may be forgiven us. For it is written, "*Blessed are they whose transgressions are forgiven, whose sins are covered. Blessed is the man unto whom the Lord shall not impute sin, and in whose mouth there is no deceit*" (Ps. xxxii. 1, 2). This blessing[6] is upon all who have been elected by God through Jesus Christ our Lord, to whom be glory for ever and ever. Amen.

LI. For all the acts of sin we have committed after any of the attacks[7] of the enemy, let us entreat that pardon may be extended to us; and moreover, all who came forward as leaders in dissension and variance should have

---

[1] Common, lit. "common to human nature" (ἀνθρώπινος); the same word as, in 1 Cor. x. 13, is translated "common to man."

[2] *i. e.* at the last day.

[3] This quotation is drawn in part from Is. xxvi. 20 (cf. Matt. vi. 6), and in part from Ezek. xxxvii. 12.

[4] This word (ταμεῖα) is translated in Matt. xxiv. 26, "secret chambers."

[5] Lit. "blessed were we." The writer throws his thought forward into the hereafter, and finds himself looking back to this present time, and recognizing how "blessed we were, if we obeyed."

[6] The same quotation occurs in Rom. iv. 7, 8, followed by "Cometh this blessedness upon the circumcision only?" This passage is evidently a reminiscence.

[7] The Latin version supplies the word missing in the Greek "incursiones."

regard for our common hope. For they that walk in fear and love would rather that sufferings should befall themselves than their neighbours; they would involve themselves in condemnation sooner than that concord which has been handed down to them so nobly and righteously.

Better is it that a man should make confession of his transgressions than that he should harden his heart, as did they who divided themselves against Moses the servant [1] of God. For their judgment was made manifest, in that they went down alive into Hades, where "*Death shall be their shepherd*" (Ps. xlix. 14). For no other reason were Pharaoh and his host and the princes of Egypt, "*their chariots and their riders*" (Ex. xv. 19) engulfed in the Red Sea and destroyed, than because their foolish hearts were hardened, after that the signs and the wonders had been shown in the land of Egypt by the hand of Moses the servant of God.

LII. The Master of the Universe, brethren, stands in need of nothing besides;[2] there is nothing that He asks from any man, save that he should make confession unto Him. For the elect David says: "*I will confess unto the Lord, and it shall please Him better than a bullock that hath horns and hoofs: let the poor see it and be glad*" (Ps. lxix. 30—32). And again he says: "*Offer unto God a sacrifice of praise, and pay unto the Most High thy vows: and call upon Me in the day of thine affliction; I will deliver thee, and thou shalt glorify Me. For a sacrifice unto God is a broken spirit*" (Ps. l. 14, 15).

LIII. But ye know and know well, beloved, the sacred

---

[1] A and S have "servant," C has "man of God." The Latin version supports A and S, reading "famulum."

[2] This translation is in accord with the Syriac, but is not that of the Latin version, which takes τῶν ἁπάντων with ἀπροσδεής.

Scriptures, and ye have examined into the oracles of God; it is to put you in remembrance that we thus write. For when Moses went up into the mount, and had passed forty days and forty nights in fasting and humiliation, God spake unto him: "*Moses, Moses,*[1] *get thee down quickly from hence, for thy people which thou didst bring forth out of Egypt have transgressed; they are quickly turned aside out of the way which thou commandedst them; they have made them molten images.*" Furthermore the Lord spake unto him: "*I have spoken unto thee once and yet again, saying, 'I have seen this people, and behold it is a stiff-necked people: let Me alone, that I may destroy them, and I will blot out their name from under heaven: and I will make of thee a nation strong and wonderful and greater than it*'" (Deut. ix. 12—14). And Moses said, "*Not so, Lord; forgive this people their sin, or blot me also out of the book of the living*" (Ex. xxxii. 32). What mighty love! What surpassing perfection! What boldness of speech in the servant to his Lord, when he prays that the multitude may be forgiven, or else asks that he himself may be blotted out with them.

LIV. Who then among you is noble? who is compassionate? who is filled with love? Let him say, "If I am the cause of variance and strife and divisions, I withdraw; I will depart whithersoever ye will; I am prepared to obey the commands of the people. Only let the flock of Christ be in peace under its appointed presbyters." Let a man do this, and he shall win for himself a great name in Christ, and every place will welcome him; "*for the earth is the Lord's, and the ful-*

---

[1] These words, "Moses, Moses," do not occur in the original, or in the Syriac version, or in the Latin version. As they appear in the two Greek MSS., A and C, it is quite probable that they are copied from the form of the quotation as it appears in the Epistle of Barnabas twice, §§ 4 and 14.

ness thereof."[1] This is the course that ever was, and will be adopted by those who live the life of citizens in the kingdom of God, a life which is not to be repented of.

LV. But let us bring forward the examples of Gentiles also. Many kings and princes, in the time of some sore pestilence, have been led by an oracle to give themselves over to death,[2] if so they might deliver their people at the cost of their own blood. Many have withdrawn from their own cities, in order to bring divisions to an end.[3] We know that many among ourselves have delivered themselves over to bondage,[4] in order to ransom others. Many have voluntarily entered into slavery,[4] and have fed others with the price received for themselves. Many women have been strengthened by the grace of God to perform many manly deeds. The blessed Judith, when her city was besieged, begged leave of the elders to be allowed to go out into the camp of the strangers. Thus in face of danger she went forth for love of her country and of her besieged people, and the Lord delivered Holofernes[5] into the hand of a woman. Equally great was the danger to which Esther, who was made perfect in her faith, exposed herself, in order that she might save the twelve tribes of Israel from their extreme peril:[6] for by

---

[1] "A noble application of Ps. xxiv. 1. He retires in God's cause, and there is room for him everywhere on God's earth" (Lightfoot).

[2] Cf. Codrus, King of Athens, of whom Horace wrote (*Odes* iii. 19), "Codrus pro patria non timidus mori." He was warned by an oracle that Athens would never fall if its ruler perished by the hand of the invaders, and so he entered the enemy's camp in disguise, and provoked a quarrel with a foreigner, who killed him.

[3] *e.g.* Lycurgus, the Spartan legislator.

[4] We have no recorded instances of such acts of generosity; it is probable that such deeds as are referred to were performed by Christians, if we are to judge from the words "among ourselves."

[5] Cf. Judith xiii. 7.

[6] Cf. Esther vii.

her fasting and humiliation she entreated the all-surveying Master, the God of all the ages. And He saw the humility of her soul, and delivered the people for whose sake she had incurred danger.

LVI. Therefore let us also intercede for those who are in any transgression, and let us pray that reasonableness[1] and humility may be given to them, in order that they may render submission, not to us, but to the will of God. For thus they shall be remembered with thoughts of compassion before God and the Church, and their memorial shall come to maturity and bring forth fruit. Let us accept chastening, beloved, at which no man ought to repine. The correction which we offer one to another is good and highly profitable : for it binds us to the will of God. For thus saith the holy Word : "*The Lord hath chastened me sore, but He hath not given me over unto death. For whom the Lord loveth He chasteneth, and scourgeth every son whom He receiveth. For the righteous,*" it saith, "*shall chasten me in mercy and reprove me, but let not the oil[2] of sinners anoint my head*" (Ps. cxviii. 18 ; Prov. iii. 12 ; Ps. cxli. 5). And again He saith, "*Blessed is the man whom the Lord hath reproved, and refuse not the correction of the Almighty ; for He giveth pain, and restoreth again ; He woundeth, and His hands make whole. Six times shall He take thee out of troubles, and in the seventh there shall no evil touch thee. In famine He shall save thee from death, and in war from the hand of the sword. And from the scourge of the tongue shall He hide thee, and thou shalt not be afraid when evils arise against thee. Thou shalt laugh to scorn the unright-*

---

[1] Reasonableness. This is one of the key-words of the Epistle.
[2] The Latin version, which reads "oleum," confirms C which has ἔλεον (for ἔλαιον), the reading of the Septuagint, as against A which has ἔλεος (for ἔλαιος), which would have no meaning here.

eous and the transgressors, and thou shalt not be afraid of wild beasts; for the beasts of the field shall be at peace with thee. Then shalt thou know that thy house shall be at peace, and the abode of thy tent shall not fail, and thou shalt know that thy seed shall be great, and thy children as the rich verdure of the field. And thou shalt come to thy grave as ripe corn that is reaped in his season, and as a heap of corn in the threshing-floor that is gathered in its ripeness" (Job v. 17—26).

Consider, beloved, what protection there is for such as be chastened by the Master; for in that He is a kind Father, He chastens us that we may find mercy through His holy chastening.

LVII. Ye therefore, that created the division, submit to your presbyters,[1] and receive chastening unto repentance, bowing the knees of your heart. Learn to be in subjection; put away from you that proud and overbearing masterfulness of speech. Better is it that your name should be recorded in the flock of Christ, however mean your position, than that ye should be held in high repute and yet be cast out from your hope in Him. For thus saith the All-virtuous Wisdom,[2] *"Behold, I will pour out the speech of my spirit upon you, and I will teach you my word. For I was calling, and ye obeyed not; I was holding out words and ye heeded not: but ye set at nought my counsels, and disobeyed my reproofs. Therefore I also will laugh at your destruction, and will mock at you when calamity cometh upon you, and when distress seizeth you suddenly, and when your desolation falleth upon you like a whirlwind, and infliction and invasion beset you. For it*

---

[1] The Latin version, which in §§ 1, 44, and 55 has rightly translated πρεσβύτεροι by "seniores," and in § 54 by "presbiteri," here renders it "seniores." If it is right, the "seniores" may be the members of the Church in Rome, who are appealing for peace.

[2] The Book of the Proverbs of Solomon.

shall be that, when ye call upon me, I will not hear you. Wicked men shall seek me, but they shall not find me; for they hated wisdom and chose not the fear of the Lord; they would not heed my counsels, but scorned my reproofs. Therefore they shall eat the fruits of their own way, and shall be filled[1] *with their own ungodliness. For in that they wronged the simple, they shall be slain, and judgment shall destroy the ungodly. But whoso hearkeneth unto me shall dwell in confidence and hope, and shall be quiet without fear of any evil"* (Prov. i. 23—33).

LVIII. Let us therefore give ear to His all-holy and glorious Name; let us flee from those warnings we have heard, which Wisdom pronounces against the disobedient, that so we may dwell in peace with full confidence in the most holy Name of His majesty. Receive our counsel, and ye will not repent of it. For as God liveth, and our Lord Jesus Christ liveth, and the Holy Spirit, in Whom are the faith and hope of the elect, verily there is a recompense for him that with lowliness and determined reasonableness[2] shall give himself with his whole heart[3] to perform the commands and ordinances of God: he shall have his place, and his name shall be written in the number of those who are saved through Jesus Christ, through whom is glory unto God for ever and ever. Amen.

LIX. But if any be disobedient to the words that God hath spoken by us,[4] let them know that they will

---

[1] At this point A fails us, leaf 168 having been lost. It was only when the MS. of Bryennius (C) was published in 1875, that the substance of the next six chapters came to be known.

[2] This phrase is a paradox, as appears more plainly in the Greek; perhaps "unyielding conciliation" would show the playful contradiction more clearly. It occurs again in § 62.

[3] With his whole heart, lit. without any feeling of hesitation or regret.

[4] Notice the remarkable claim made by the Roman elders. Cf.

be guilty of a serious fault and will incur no small danger, but we shall be guiltless in respect of this sin. And it shall be our prayer with earnest entreaty and supplication, that the Creator of the universe will preserve inviolate the number of His elect that has been numbered throughout the whole world,[1] through His beloved Son Jesus Christ,[2] by whom He called us from darkness to light, and from wilful ignorance to the knowledge of the glory of His Name.

Grant unto us,[3] O Lord, that we may rest our hope

---

§ 63, where the Latin version makes it clear that we should thus translate, "the advice which by the Holy Spirit we have written unto you."

[1] The thought of the scattering of the people of God throughout the world, of their preservation by God, and their gathering together again is one of the most familiar liturgical touches which occur in early writings. It is undoubtedly borrowed from a Jewish source, having probably been commonly employed in the worship of the synagogue. Cf. 2 Maccabees ii. 18 (R.V.), "In God have we hope, that He will quickly have mercy upon us, and gather us together out of all the earth into the holy place." We find the same thought in the *Doctrine of the Apostles*, § 10 (Bigg, p. 64), "Remember, Lord, Thy Church, to deliver her from all evil, and to perfect her in Thy love, and gather together from the four winds her that is sanctified into Thy kingdom which Thou didst prepare for her." Again, *Doctrine*, § 9, "As this bread that is broken was scattered upon the mountains, and gathered together and became one, so let Thy Church be gathered together from the ends of the earth into Thy kingdom."

[2] Here we have another interesting liturgical reminiscence. We find the expression Ἰησοῦς (Χριστὸς), παῖς ἀγαπητός, or ἠγαπημένος, or παῖς alone, in this passage, in the *Doctrine*, § 10, and in the *Passion* of Polycarp, § 14, and in each case it is connected with the giving of increased knowledge. In the *Doctrine*, § 10, we find, "We give Thee thanks, Holy Father . . . for the knowledge and faith and immortality, which Thou hast made known unto us through Thy Son Jesus." Again in the *Passion*, we find, "Father of Thy beloved . . . Son Jesus Christ, through whom we have received the knowledge of Thee."

[3] The Latin version serves but to confirm the reading of C and S, translating ἐλπίζειν by "sperare." It would be harsh to make ἐλπίζειν depend upon ἐκάλεσεν, and begin a new and irregular

on that Name of Thine whence all creation springs; do Thou open the eyes of our heart that we may know Thee, who alone "*abidest Most High in the high place, Holy in the holy place;*[1] *who humblest the arrogance of the proud; who bringest the counsels of the nations to nought; who liftest up the humble and bringest down them that are set on high; who makest rich and makest poor; who killest and makest alive;*" who alone art the Benefactor of spirits and the God of all flesh; "*who searchest into the abysses;*" who surveyest the works of men; who art the Helper of them that are in danger, "*the Saviour of them that are in despair,*" the Creator and Overseer of every spirit; who multipliest peoples on the earth, and hast chosen out from them all those that love Thee, through Jesus Christ Thy beloved Son, through Whom Thou dost correct us, sanctify us, and honour us.

We call upon Thee, O Master, to be "*our helper and defender*" (Ps. cxix. 114). Save such of us as are in affliction; have pity on the humble; raise up the fallen; show Thyself to such as are in want; heal the sick;[2] convert those of Thy people that are in error; feed the hungry; ransom our prisoners; raise up the feeble; comfort the weak-hearted.[3] "*Let all the Gentiles know that Thou art God alone*" (1 Kings viii. 60), and that Jesus Christ is Thy Son, and that "*we are Thy people and the sheep of Thy pasture*" (Ps. c. 3).

---

sentence with ἀνοίξας. We must therefore accept Lightfoot's suggestion, which, by inserting "Grant to us, O Lord," makes excellent sense, and restores the construction of the sentence.

[1] The next few lines are a series of short quotations from Is. lvii. 15, and xiii. 11; Job v. 11; Is. x. 33; 1 Sam. ii. 7; Deut. xxxii. 39; Ecclus. xvi. 18, 19, and Judith ix. 11.

[2] ἀσεβεῖς C; but the Syriac version gives "ægrotos," and the La in "infirmos," and therefore Gebhardt's conjecture, ἀσθενεῖς, seems fully justified.

[3] Cf. 1 Thess. v. 14.

LX. Thou didst manifest the perpetual constitution of the universe by Thy works therein. Thou, O Lord, didst create the world; Thou art faithful throughout all generations, Thou are righteous in Thy judgments, Thou art wonderful in Thy strength and splendour, Thou art wise to create, and cunning to establish the things that are made, Thou art good in Thy works which are seen, and faithful with such as put their confidence in Thee, Thou art merciful and full of compassion. O! do Thou forgive us our transgressions and our unrighteousnesses and our faults and our weaknesses. Impute not to Thy servants and Thine handmaids all their sin, but cleanse us throughly by Thy truth, and *direct our steps* that we may walk *in holiness* and righteousness and simplicity *of heart*, and that we may *do that which is good and well-pleasing in the sight* of Thee and of our rulers [1] (Ps. cxix. 133; Deut. xiii. 18). Yea, Lord, *cause Thy face to shine upon us for blessing* (Ps. lxvii. 1) with peace, that we may be covered *by Thy mighty hand*, and be delivered from all sin *by Thy high arm* (Ex. vi. 1). Save us from them that hate us without a cause. Grant peace and concord to us and to all that dwell upon the earth, as Thou gavest it unto our fathers, when they called upon Thee in faith and truth with holiness, that we may obey [2] Thy almighty and all-holy Name, and render submission to our rulers and governors upon the earth.[3]

---

[1] ἄρχοντες, *i. e.* our temporal rulers.
[2] Lightfoot and others make an insertion in order to restore the construction, not being satisfied with the loose accusative; but although it is slightly rough, yet it is quite allowable, and has the advantage of the direct support of the Latin version, which reads "obœdientes."
[3] The Latin version comes to our aid again here. All editors previous to Lightfoot had connected all the words after "all-holy Name" with "Thou hast given" at the beginning of § 61. Dr. Hort suggested the new punctuation to Lightfoot, and the change has

LXI. Thou, O Master, by Thy mighty and unspeakable power hast given unto them the authority to rule, that we may recognize the honour and glory that Thou hast given them, and may submit ourselves to them, in obedience to Thy will. Do Thou grant unto them, O Lord, health, peace, concord, and security, that they may exercise without hindrance the lordship which Thou hast committed into their hands. For Thou, O Master which art in heaven, King of the ages, dost give unto the sons of men honour and glory and dominion over the things that are upon the earth. Do Thou, Lord, direct their counsel according to that which is good and well-pleasing in Thy sight, in order that by a godly exercise of the power that Thou hast committed unto them in a spirit of peace and meekness, they may win Thy favour. O Thou, who alone art able to give us these gifts and yet other blessings in greater abundance, we give thanks unto Thee through Jesus Christ, the High Priest and Protector of our souls, through Whom be glory and majesty unto Thee both now and for all generations and for evermore. Amen.

LXII. We have written fully unto you, brethren, concerning those things that belong to our religion, and those that are most helpful to all such as seek to live virtuously[1] in holiness and righteousness. For as touching faith and repentance and genuine love and moderation and self-restraint and patience, we have dealt with every

---

been entirely justified by the Latin, which leaves the matter beyond the region of doubt. The words "rulers and governors" now recall naturally "our rulers" a few lines before, while § 61 begins with the emphatic "Thou," with which § 60 began.

[1] The Latin version goes to show that ἐνάρετον βίον is accusative after διευθύνειν (which the Syriac also indicates), and that, this not being understood, εἰς was inserted so as to connect the words with ὠφελιμωτάτων.

point, and have reminded you how necessary it is that ye should please Almighty God by a holy life of righteousness and truth and longsuffering, and how ye ought with determined reasonableness to live harmoniously in love and peace, forgetting all past injuries. For it was by their humility that our fathers of whom we have written found favour not only with God their Father and Creator but also with all men. And so much the more gladly did we recall these duties to your memory, as we were assured that we were writing to men who were faithful and well-established, and had examined into the oracles of the discipline of God.

LXIII. It is right for us therefore to pay attention to these great examples and pass beneath the yoke; let us assume the position of obedience,[1] if so we may be delivered from our foolish division, and arrive at the goal that is set before us in truth, free from any fault. For ye will afford us joy and gladness, if ye obey the advice which by the Holy Spirit we have written unto you, and put from you that unholy anger and jealousy, in answer to our appeal for concord and peace which we have addressed to you in this letter. We have sent also faithful and sober men,[2] whose life has been spent among us from youth to old age unblamably, that they may be witnesses between you and us. We do this in order that ye may know that all our thought has been, and is directed towards a speedy restoration of peace among you.

LXIV. Finally our prayer is that the All-seeing God, the Master of spirits and Lord of all flesh, who hath elected the Lord Jesus Christ and us through Him for

---

[1] After "obedience," Lightfoot inserts, retranslating from the Syriac version, "and attach ourselves to the appointed leaders of our souls," but this addition has no attestation either in C or in the Latin version, and is not needed.

[2] Cf. § 65. Claudius Ephebus and Valerius Bito.

His peculiar people, may grant unto every soul that hath called upon His mighty and holy Name,[1] faith, fear, peace, patience, longsuffering, moderation, purity, and sobriety, that it may be well-pleasing unto His Name, through Jesus Christ, our High Priest and Protector, through Whom be glory and majesty and power and honour unto Him both now and for evermore. Amen.

LXV. Send back to us speedily our envoys Claudius[2] Ephebus and Valerius[2] Bito with Fortunatus as well, in peace and joy, in order that they may the sooner bring the news of that peace and concord which we desire and pray for—in order that we too may the sooner rejoice over your return to quiet and order.

The grace of our Lord Jesus Christ be with you and with all in every place who have been called by God through Him. Through Whom be unto Him glory, honour, power, majesty, and dominion everlasting from the ages that are past for ever and ever. Amen.

---

[1] It has been suggested that we should translate ἐπικεκλημένῃ, "to every soul which is called by His Name" (cf. Gen. iv. 26 *marg.*), but the Latin version which has "invocante" decides in favour of the simpler rendering.

[2] Lightfoot, arguing from the names, Claudius and Valerius, suggests that these may have been two of the members of Cæsar's household mentioned in Phil. iv. 22.

INDEX OF SCRIPTURAL PASSAGES

	PAGE		PAGE
Genesis i. 9	39	Job xiv. 4, 5	36
,, i. 26, 27, 28	48	,, xv. 15	54
,, ii. 23	28	,, xix. 26	44
,, iv. 3–8	25	,, xxxviii. 11	39
,, xii. 1–3	30	Psalm ii. 7, 8	51
,, xiii. 14–16	31	,, iii. 5	44
,, xv. 5	47	,, xii. 3–5	34
,, xv. 5, 6	31	,, xviii. 25, 27	60
,, xviii. 27	36	,, xix. 1–3	44
Exodus ii. 14	26	,, xxii. 6, 8	36
,, iii. 11 ; iv. 10	37	,, xxiv. 1	66
,, vi. 1	73	,, xxviii. 7 (?)	44
,, xv. 19	61	,, xxxi. 18	34
,, xxxii. 32	66	,, xxxii. 1, 2	64
Numbers xii. 7	37	,, xxxii. 10	42
,, xviii. 27	46	,, xxxiv. 11-17, 19	41, 42
Deuteronomy iv. 34	46	,, xxxvii. 9, 35-37, 38	34
,, ix. 12–14	66	,, xlix. 14	61
,, xiii. 18	73	,, l. 14, 15	65
,, xiv. 2	46	,, l. 16–23	50
,, xxxii. 8, 9	45	,, li. 1–17	37, 38
,, xxxii. 39	72	,, lv. 16	26
Joshua ii. 3–5	32	,, lxii. 4	34
,, ii. 9, 13, 18, 19	32	,, lxvii. 1	73
1 Samuel ii. 7	72	,, lxix. 30–32	65
,, ii. 10	33	,, lxxviii. 36, 37	34
,, xiii. 14	37	,, lxxxix. 21	37
1 Kings viii. 60	72	,, c. 3	72
2 Chronicles xxxi. 14	46	,, civ. 4	51
Esther vii.	67	,, cx. 1	51
Job i. 1	36	,, cxviii. 18	68
,, iv. 16–18	54	,, cxviii. 19, 20	62
,, iv. 19–v. 5	54	,, cxix. 1, 4	72
,, v. 11	72	,, cxix. 133	73
,, v. 17–26	68, 69	,, cxxxix. 7, 8	45
,, xi. 2, 3	46	,, cxli. 5	68

INDEX OF SCRIPTURAL PASSAGES

	PAGE
Proverbs i. 23–33	70
,, ii. 21, 22	34
,, iii. 12	68
,, vii. 3	24
,, xx. 27	40
,, xxiv. 12	49
Isaiah iii. 5	24
,, vi. 3	49
,, x. 33	72
,, xiii. 11	72
,, xxvi. 20	64
,, xxix. 13	34
,, xl. 10	49
,, liii.	35, 36
,, lvii. 15	72
,, lix. 14	24
,, lx. 17	56
,, lxii. 11	49
,, lxvi. 2	33
Jeremiah ix. 23, 24	33
Ezekiel xxxiii. 11	29
,, xxxvii. 12	64
,, xlviii. 12	46
Daniel vii. 10	49
Habakkuk ii. 3	42
Malachi iii. 1	42
Judith ix. 11	72
,, xiii.	67
Wisdom ii. 24	25
,, xii. 12	44
Ecclesiasticus xvi. 18, 19	72
St. Matthew v. 7	33
,, vi. 14	33
,, vii. 1, 2	33
,, xiii. 3	43
,, xviii. 6	61
,, xxvi. 24	61
St. Mark ix. 42	61
,, xiv. 21	61
St. Luke vi. 31, 36–38	33
,, xvii. 1, 2	61
,, xxii. 22	61
Acts xx. 35	23
Titus iii. 1	24
Hebrews i. 3, 4	51
James iv. 6	46
1 Peter iv. 8	63

GENERAL INDEX

(The figures refer to pages)

AARON, 26, 57
Abel, 25
Abiram, 26
Abraham, 30, 31, 36, 47
Adam, 28, 64
ἀγάπη, 41
Alexandrian MS. (A), 17, 23, 24, 57, 58, 61, 63, 65, 66, 68, 70
Allegorical use of O. T., 32
Ambrose, 19
Analysis of Epistle, 14
Ananias, 60
Apollos, 61
Authorship of Epistle, 9
Azarias, 60

Barnabas, Epistle of, iv, 66
Bryennius, 17, 70

Cæsar's household, 76
Cain, 25
Canonicity of Epistle, 20
Church of Corinth, 13, 14, 22, 62
Claudius Ephebus, 76
Clement of Alexandria, 10, 18, 19, 63
Clement of Rome, 9–11
Codrus, 67
Concord, 39, 49, 55
Constantinopolitan MS. (C), 18, 23, 24, 51, 57, 58, 61, 63, 65, 66, 68, 70, 71, 72, 75
Corinth, 12
Corinthians, Epistle of St. Paul to the, 61
Cyprian, 10

Danaids, 27
Date of Epistle, 7
Dathan, 26
David, 26, 37, 65
Diaconi, 56

Dionysius of Corinth, 7, 10, 17, 26, 63
Dircæ, 27
Domitian, 8, 21
Domitilla, Flavia, 21

ἡγεμονικόν, 38
Egyptians, 37
Eldad and Modad, Prophesying of, 37, 42
Elijah, 36
Elisha, 36
Enoch, 30
ἐπιδομή, 58
ἐπιείκεια, 46, 68
Episcopi, 56, 58
ἐφόδια, 23
Esau, 25
Esther, 67
Eusebius, 7, 10, 11, 17, 20, 21
External evidence, 17
Ezekiel, 36

Flavius Clemens, 21

Gifts (Eucharistic), 59
Gnosis, 22, 62
Grabe, 36
γραφεῖον, 45

Hades, 65
Harnack, Prof., 19
Hegesippus, iii, 7, 13, 17
Heliopolis, 43
Hermas, 10
Holofernes, 67
Hort, Prof., 52, 73
Hospitality, 22, 31

Ignatius, Epistles of, iv
Irenæus, iii, 10, 11, 17

Isaac, 47

Jacob, 25, 47
Jealousy, 25 ff.
Jericho, 31
Jerome, 19
Jerusalem, 55
Jesus Christ, 33, 34 f., 40, 41, 47, 51, 52, 56, 61, 63, 66, 70, 71, 72
Job, 36
Jonah, 28
Joseph, 25
Joseph of Arimathæa, 35
Joshua, 31
Judah, 47
Judith, 67

κατοπτρίζεσθαι, 51

Laban, 47
Latin Version (L), 18, 22, 23, 24, 26, 28, 33, 35, 36, 39, 40, 48, 51, 54, 57, 58, 59, 61, 63, 64, 65, 66, 68, 69, 71, 72, 73, 74, 75, 76
Levites, 47, 54
Lightfoot, vi, 11, 23, 24, 25, 29, 33, 37, 38, 39, 40, 42, 44, 46, 49, 54, 57, 59, 63, 67, 72, 73, 75, 76
Liturgia, 55
Lot, 28, 31
Lycurgus, 67

Manuscripts of Epistle, 17
μαρτυρεῖν, 26
Miriam, 26
Misael, 60
Morin of Maredsous, Dom., 18
Moses, 25, 26, 37, 57, 65, 66

Nero, 8
Nineveh, 28
Noah, 30
Novatian, 10

Oceanus, 39
Order, 55
Origen, 10, 38, 49

παροικεῖν, 21
Paul, St., 26, 27, 61
Peter, St., 26, 27, 61
Pharaoh, 25, 65
Phœnix, 43
πίστις, 44
Polycarp, iii, iv, 7, 17, 21
  ,,   Passion of, 21, 71
Polycrates, 10
Primus, 14
Purpose of Epistle, 12

Rahab, 31, 32
Reasonableness, 46, 68, 70
Result of Epistle, 13
Resurrection, 13, 42 f., 56

Sacrifices, 55
Sanday, Prof., 19
Saul, 26
Schism, 13
Septuagint Version of O. T., 24, 25, 35, 37, 40, 45, 55, 68
Sodom, 31
Soter, Bp., 10, 20
σοφός, σοφία, 52
Spain, 27
σταθμοί, 40
Succession, 57
Syriac MS. (S), 18, 23, 24, 54, 57, 58, 63, 65, 71, 72, 74, 75

Tacitus, 43
Teaching of the Apostles, 18, 71
Trajan, 7
Translations, Era of, 19
Tübingen hypothesis, iv

Valerius Bito, 76
Victor, Bp., 10

Westcott, Bp., 41
Wordsworth, 28

Zahn, Dr., 24

χάρισμα, 52

Richard Clay & Sons, Limited, London & Bungay.

www.ingramcontent.com/pod-product-compliance
Lightning Source LLC
Chambersburg PA
CBHW020338090426
42735CB00009B/1585